IMAGES
of Scotland

CELTIC
FOOTBALL CLUB
1887-1967

Brother Walfrid, the force behind Celtic's founding in 1887.

IMAGES
of Scotland

CELTIC
FOOTBALL CLUB
1887-1967

Compiled by
Tom Campbell and Pat Woods

TEMPUS

First published 1998
Copyright © Tom Campbell and Pat Woods, 1998

Tempus Publishing Limited
The Mill, Brimscombe Port,
Stroud, Gloucestershire, GL5 2QG

ISBN 0 7524 1565 4

Typesetting and origination by
Tempus Publishing Limited
Printed in Great Britain by
Midway Clark Printing, Wiltshire

For all the relatives of Pat Woods, and for Pauline, Robin and Dana.

For the members of the following supporters' clubs: the Lisbon Lions (Glasgow), the North Wales Emerald, and the Edinburgh No.1.

Jock Stein

Contents

Introduction   7

1.   1887-1918   9

2.   1918-1945   33

3.   1945-1965   63

4.   1965-1967   111

Willie Maley played in Celtic's first match against Rangers and served Celtic as match secretary before emerging as manager (and secretary) until his 'retirement' in 1940. His contribution to the club ranks close to that of Jock Stein. "The only instruction the team got from the tall autocrat in the grey hombarg hat – the great Willie Malley – was: 'Go out and win – or else!' " (Matt Lynch, ex-Celt)

Acknowledgements

We wish to thank the following for their assistance and the use of photographs and other material: the Daily Express, the Daily Record and Sunday Mail, Express Newspapers, Scottish Media Group Newspapers, D.C. Thomson Ltd, the Celtic Supporters' Association, Richard Fearon, Matt Lynch, Robert McElroy, Matilda Madden, Jack Murray, Tom O'Neill, and Eric Shannon.

Our thanks are also due to Matthew Forlow in his role as editor, and Keith Laidlaw for his patience and expertize as a lay-out consultant.

Every effort has been made to identify and acknowledge as above the source of the illustrations used in this book.

This is an independent publication, prepared without any involvement on the part of Celtic Football Club.

Introduction

Celtic Football Club was founded in November 1887, and played its first match almost seven months later against a side representing Rangers. The 'friendly' – won 5-2 by the new club – was played on the first Celtic Park, a stadium that had been a six-acre vacant lot at the founding. The site had been transformed into an acceptable ground for the occasion, consisting of an open-air stand, a raised terracing and a level grassy playing surface.

Significantly, the transformation had been accomplished largely by the voluntary labour of many in Glasgow's expanding Irish and Catholic community, and that is what makes Celtic a unique Scottish institution.

The origins of the club are rooted in that community and were charitable in nature. Brother Walfrid, the main force behind Celtic's founding, saw that money had to be raised to keep body and soul together in the needy parishes of Glasgow's East End. He was aware of the enthusiasm for football among the working-class and noted the success of a Catholic club (Hibernian) in winning the Scottish Cup in 1887. A similar club in Glasgow with its larger Irish community could raise considerable sums for charity. Walfrid was helped in his campaign by a coterie of hard-working businessmen (all Irish and Catholic) who had emerged as leaders of their community.

Survival as a football club was not guaranteed and that fact brought the first moral dilemma for Celtic. Scottish football was in its infancy and nominally amateur, but most clubs induced talented players to join them and paid them illegally from the start. Celtic had to adopt this practice and were masters at recruitment as Hibernian found out to their cost.

Celtic were a prime attraction and major success on the field eventually came their way. Many followers of the sport were drawn to the new club's dashing approach, but the vast majority of the club's support came from the Irish and Catholic communities across Scotland. This immigrant class had a hard life in industrial Scotland through a lack of education and discrimination practised against them by the native population. The success of Celtic on the playing field gave that community comfort and hope for a better future.

That success quickly posed another dilemma. Record crowds produced vast sums in revenue, and donations to the charities designated by Brother Walfrid, but 'amateur' players were demanding higher remuneration and a new and larger stadium had to be built. The Scottish League was also formed in 1890 and the legalisation of professional players was recognised in 1893. Could Celtic survive as a charitable trust in such an era of expansion? The debate within the club was heartfelt and spirited but in 1897 Celtic became a limited liability company. Despite that move to commercialism the support among the bedrock communities never wavered and it could be argued that the club's original charitable impulse never did die out completely.

Celtic played a leading role in every aspect of the development of football within Scotland during those formative years. They were the prime movers in the campaign to establish the Scottish League and the inevitable sequel - the legalising of professionalism in Scotland. By 1918 Celtic could lay a valid claim to being 'the best football club in Britain'. The record on the field was incomparable: fourteen Scottish League Championships and nine Scottish Cups won, while the accomplishments in other areas were equally impressive. The modern stadium, capable of holding 70,000 spectators, was selected frequently to host international fixtures as well as World Cycling Championships and regular athletic meetings.

Some Scots resented Celtic's pre-eminence and any patriot looking for a Scottish side to back against 'the Irish upstarts' would have to settle on Rangers. The other Glasgow club had emerged as Celtic's closest rival for football honours but the rivalry was waged on other fronts; for example, the competition to secure such lucrative fixtures as the international matches and cup finals was intense.

The rivalry took on a more sinister hue with an increase in sectarianism among the clubs' followers. Celtic had been essentially an Irish club from the start, and Rangers a Scottish one; Celtic's founders had been Catholic, and Rangers', presumably, Protestant. Some commentators have traced the increase in hostility to a huge influx of Belfast shipworkers to Clydeside, and these men gravitated towards Rangers as the club to follow. At much the same time the administration of the Govan club embarked upon a strict, if unstated, policy of 'No Catholics'. Ironically, Celtic had become increasingly a Scottish club and less an Irish one.

The most unfortunate aspect of Rangers' policy was that for the next thirty years they were the most successful side in Scotland, especially dominant in the league championship. Nobody in the general public would want to quarrel with success. Celtic between the Wars were eclipsed in every aspect of football. A small group of men was in charge of the club and were content, it appeared, to accept reasonable share-dividends and to assume the status that a directorship in Celtic conferred. Two examples of their short-sightedness could be cited: the reserve side was disbanded in the early 1920s as an economic measure, and in 1929 they attempted to sell Jimmy McGrory to Arsenal for a British record fee in order to pay for the building of the new grandstand.

During the Second World War, Celtic as a football club made little effort to entertain their supporters and the malaise continued for some years after 1945. There were sporadic attempts to improve the situation. For example, after the narrow escape from relegation in 1948 the chairman Bob Kelly arranged for a new coach to help with the training. Jimmy Hogan came to Scotland with a European reputation and the sprightly 70 year-old did effect some improvements, but the club was hampered by the fatal combination of a weak manager (Jimmy McGrory) and a dictatorial chairman. The successes were few but memorable - a Coronation Cup triumph in 1953, a League and Cup double in 1954, and a memorable rout of Rangers by 7-1 in the 1957 League Cup Final. After that victory, achieved by an ageing side, Celtic persisted in a youth policy for too long and accomplished nothing for seven years.

In 1965 Jock Stein was brought back as manager, and this broke another barrier as the new man was not a Catholic, unlike Celtic's three previous managers (Willie Maley, Jimmy McStay and Jimmy McGrory). It was not an issue with the supporters who craved success on the pitch and who respected Stein as a former club captain and coach. Where McGrory had been weak, Stein was strong. He imposed a firm discipline on his football squad, established a playing-method which suited the talents of his players and insisted on control over all aspects of the football side. His supreme gift was an ability to inspire his charges with legitimate self-belief and to communicate his ideas to them, his message re-enforced with a commanding physical presence.

Celtic once more assumed the leading role in Scottish football and went further than that. Dominant at home, in 1967 Celtic became the first British club to win the European Cup and did so with style and flair. The seasons between 1965 and 1970 saw Celtic again as a model for the football world.

One

1887-1917

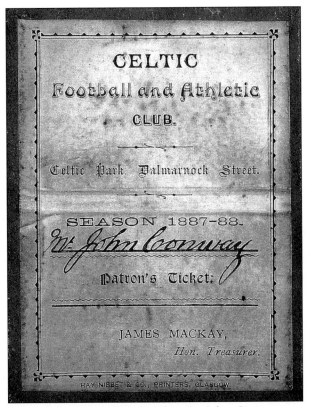

The first membership card for Celtic FC, issued to Dr John Conway, a much loved medical practitioner, who became honorary president.

old friends, the Blackburn Rovers, over their dreaded foes, the Accrington. As the match took place at Accrington, it was generally feared that the Rovers were in for a sure drop. But the old spirit has evidently re-animated the thrice-holders of the English cup, and they came out of a most uncertain fight with a 3-to-1 victory. It really does look as if the Rovers were going again to slip into first honours. The West Bromwich Albion have considerable credit in emerging successfully from their tie with the Wolverhampton Wanderers, a club who, last year, gave the ultimate winners the severest stretch they received during the entire competition. It is a pity we never see the Throstles in their true form when they visit Scotland. North End didn't take long to munch Everton's toffy, which had proved such a stubborn *rock* of offence to the once-mighty Bolton Wanderers. Their 6-to-1 victory only emphasises the distance they still tower above their dear friends from the trotter town.

The Clydesdale Harriers are arranging confined section hcps. for the badge given by the club. The main body have also decided to have a confined 7 miles hcp. at Chryston on 7th January. There will also be a "section championship" competition on 21st January next, probably at Paisley, the distance being 8 miles, open to teams of 10 from each section—headquarters, however, supplying two teams—the first 5 to count, on the same lines as the cross-country championship. On the same afternoon there will also be a 300 yds. hcp., for which there should be a good entry. Now then, gentlemen, get into form at once, for these interesting events which are before you. We are sure that every Clydesdale Harrier will be pleased to hear that Mr. William Brown has been promoted to the responsible position of president of the club, vacated by Mr. Mackintosh, while Mr. Mellish replaces Mr. Brown in the vice-president's chair. These appointments are a guarantee that at least equal enterprise will be shown in the management of the club in the future, both being enthusiasts.

and Robertson being chosen. The latter, we feel sure, could not have been overlooked, as by his form against Bradford and other clubs, he showed himself to be quite capable of being tried. We confess to some chagrin at White not being included, more so as we were the first to bring his name before public notice. Chambers' selection as back will meet with general approval. He has developed into a first-class man, and as "Tackler" remarked last week, in his present form he is fit to play in any match. It is also gratifying to note that the same writer's opinion regarding Marsh and Wilson has met with such hearty approval. Regarding the reserve, "We want to know" (in the language of Goschen) why Brown, of the St. George, has not a place, and why Ralston and Crawford are compared to him? The answers would likely be as prolific and as satisfactory as those which the fighting politician gets to the thousand and one he asks in a session.

The Southern Athletic Club, a very excellent agency in connection with the Southern Section of the Young Men's Christian Association, are determined to improve their position in the athletic world, and, as a first move, desire to secure private ground. They have, with the object of raising funds for this laudable purpose, arranged a high class dramatic entertainment, to take place in the South Side Assembly Rooms, on Tuesday evening next, and to be carried through by the Athenæum Dramatic Club, under the direction of Mr. Walter Baynham, F.E.I.S. We are assured of the excellent quality of the bill of fare, and only hope that the attendance may be large and appreciative.

We learn that the efforts which have lately been made to organise in Glasgow a first-class Catholic football club, have been successfully consummated by the formation of the "Glasgow Celtic Football and Athletic Club," under influential auspices. They have secured a six-acre ground in the east-end, which they mean to put in fine order. We wish the "Celts" all success.

The Australian cricketers who are to visit England will leave the Colonies about the middle of March.

Applications for fixtures have already been sent to Mr. Alcock from Scotland.

The Parsee Cricketers are to commence their tour of 1888 in England on June 8.

The annual meeting of county secretaries is to be held at Lords on Tuesday, December 6, at noon.

It will be satisfactory to the general body of English cricketers to learn that an agreement has been come to between those who are responsible for the management of the two English teams now in the Colonies, to combine with a view to place the pick of the two parties in the field to meet the cream of Australian cricket.

The village of Renton was brimful with excitement on Saturday, when the result of the Hearts v. Saints tie was made known.

The excitement has now risen to a fever heat. Renton would sooner have gone to Edinburgh, where they have a lot of supporters, than show face at Westmarch.

At any rate they will require to play all they know if the Saints are to be defeated.

The Tontinites should have met Dumbarton at Boghead last Saturday, but owing to the state of the weather the match was declared off.

The Renton lads meanwhile took advantage of the opportunity to see the struggle at Cathkin, which they did with satisfaction.

If you want to see this year's international goalkeeper, just cast your eyes on J. Lindsay.

Little M'Nee purposes making a strong bid for his cap this year also.

The Rangers have scored 9 goals during the past month, and they have met 3rd L.R.V., Cowlairs, Battlefield, and Port-Glasgow Athletic. That certainly looks like a revival of form.

The Q.P. have scored 9 goals during the past month and lost 2. The 3rd L.R.V. have just reversed the figures—lost 9 goals and won 3. There must be a pulling up out Cathkin way.

It is rather a strange coincidence that the Hibs. have during each of the last three months scored three wins to one loss.

The connection between football and charity may not be at once obvious to everybody, and it might be interesting to indicate how this connection was brought about. For many years the members of the St Vincent de Paul Society in the East-End had worked quietly and steadily to relieve the poverty and suffering in the district, but the claims upon the society far exceeded the slender sums at its disposal, and the members began to look around for some source of income yet undiscovered. The Edinburgh Hibs, who that year had won the Scottish Cup, were asked to play a charity match against Clyde at old Barrowfield Park, Bridgeton. The move was pleasingly successful, and the then wonderful sum of £50 was realised after all expenses had been paid. This happy windfall placed football in a new light, and some of the far-seeing members of the St Vincent de Paul said—"If £50 can be raised by a single game between strange teams, why should we not have a team of our own, and the surplus profits divided among local charities?" Thus it came about that on 6th November, 1887, the Celtic F.C. was formally constituted at a meeting in St Mary's Hall, East Rose Street, Glasgow. Having put their hands to the plough, the promoters lost no time in getting to work, and a week later — November 13th — ground was leased in Dalmarnock Street, Parkhead. Of course, this meant money, and subscriptions were asked for, and ready response was made, the first subscriber being Rev. Father Van der Heyde, a Dutch curate in St Mary's, under the late Canon Carmichael. Of course, it should be understood that the originator of the club, and the mainstay of its early days, was the late Rev.

Bro. Walfrid, the then head of the Marist Brothers of Glasgow. Bro. Walfrid did more to start the club and set it on its feet than any other man, and, among the Old Guard who still survive, the name of the popular Marist is held in affection and his memory is ever green. It seems that the choice of club colours gave food for argument and much discussion, and it was only after long consideration that the present colours, green and white, were chosen.

No fanfare surrounded the announcement of Celtic's birth.

The *Glasgow Observer* (a Catholic newspaper) of 25 June 1927 contained the first in a five-part history of Celtic. The author is unequivocal about the role played by Brother Walfrid in the club's origins.

OPENING OF CELTIC FOOTBALL
AND ATHLETIC PARK,
DALMARNOCK STREET, PARKHEAD.
GRAND OPENING MATCH.
HIBERNIANS (EDINBURGH)
V.
COWLAIRS.

TO-DAY (EXHIBITION DAY), MAY 8TH. Kick-off at 6 P.M. prompt. Admission, 6d. Ladies Free. Grand Stand 6d. extra each Person. N.B.—The park is two minutes' walk from the Parkhead and London Road Tramcar and Railway Stations.

Hibernian and Cowlairs (the latter soon to be defunct) provided the teams for the first match to be held at the new ground on 8 May 1888.

LIST OF CLUBS.

CONTRACTIONS.—*Ground*—P, Park. *Colours*—s j, striped jersey ; s s, striped shirt ; v s j, vertical striped jersey ; v s s, vertical striped shirt ; k, knickers ; s, shirt ; bk, black ; bl, blue ; w, white ; h, halved.

GLASGOW AND SUBURBS.

CLUB.	GROUND.	COLOURS.	HON. SECRETARY.	MATCH SECRETARY.
Battlefield - -	Mossfield, Titwood	black and white s j -		James Cunninghame, Vale View-ter., Langside
Celtic - - -	Celtic Park - -	green and white - -	J. O'Hara, 77 East Rose-st., Glasgow	W Maley, Argyle place, New Cathcart
Do. 2nd XI.	Do.	Do.		James Curtis, 5 Bowling Green-ter., Bridgeton
Clyde - - -	Barrowfield Park -	red & bk s j, dark bl k	T. Anderson, 77 Main-st., Bridgeton	R. Young, 38 Old Dalmarnock-road, Bridgeton
Cowlairs - -	Gourlay P., Springb'n	white shirt, blue k -	G. Henderson, 529 Springburn-road	J. Halley, 107 Bothwell-street
Glasgow Temp. Ath.	Saracen P., Possilp'k	bl and w v s s, bl k -	A. M'Lauchlan, 11 Tillie-street -	Peter F. Paul, 408 Parliamentary-road
Glasgow University	Gilmorehill -	bk j, gold badge, w k		G. Phillips, 2 Westercraigs, Dennistoun
Govan Athletic	Moore Park, Govan	bk and white s j, blue k	W. Hanna, 18 Harmony-row, Govan	Harry Wilson, 481 Govan-road, Govan
Kelvinside Athletic	G. U. Y. M. C. A. A. C. P	white s and blue k -	D. D. Warren, 162 Gt. Western-road	John D. Martin, 7 Rupert street
Linthouse -	Langlands P., Govan	navy blue j and k -	J. Walker, Jr., 3 Helen st., Govan	J. Woodrow, 135 Cumberland-st., S.S.
Maryhill - - -	Kelvinvale Park -	w & bl perpendicular s and dk bl k	John Hunter, 72 Main-st., Maryhill	Charles Griffin, jun., 19 Gairbraid-avenue, Maryhill
Northern - -	Hydepark, Springb'n	light & dark bl h j, w k	T. Moir, 389 Springburn-rd, Springb'n	W. Mackay, 47 Renfrew-street
Partick Thistle -	Inchview, Whiteinch	navy blue j and k -	A. M. Smith, 6 Church-st., Partick	J. Suter, 7 Downanhill-street, Partick
Do. Swifts	Do.	Do.		A. M. Smith, 6 Church-st., Partick
Pollokshields Ath. -	Pollok Park -	white jersey - -	James Love, 33 Renfrew-st., Glasgow	James Love, 33 Renfrew-st , Glasgow
Queen's Park -	Hampden Park -	black and white s j -	Wm. Berry, 24 Queen-street -	Geo. Gilles, 137 West Regent-street
Do. Strollers	Do.	Do.		Geo. B. Neil, 11 Hampden-terrace, Mount Florida
Do. Hampden XI.	Do.	Do.		S. Wylie, 24 Dixon-avenue, Crosshill
Rangers - -	Ibrox Park, Ibrox	royal blue s, white k	D. B. M'Conechy, 14 Willowbank-cres.	J. Gossland, 106 Claythorn-street
Do. Swifts	Do.	Do.		J. M. Grant, 48 Overnewton-st., West
Do. Ibrox XI.	Do.	Do.		George Denny, 24 Kelvin-drive
Southern Athletic -	Moray P., Strathb'ngo	blue & white s j, blue k	James Kirkland, 21 Warwick-street	H. A. Mackay, 82 Houston-st., S.S.
Shettleston -	Carntyne Park -	red and white s j -	T. Clachan, Sandyhill-cottage	W. Dodds, 432 Neilston-ter., Parkhead
Thistle - -	Beechwood Park -	blue & white s j, blue k	W. L. Gray, Howe Machine Co., Bridgeton	R. Lockhart, 46 Gilmour-st., Oatlands, S.S.
United Abstainers -	Victoria P., Crosshill	bl & gold v s j, white k	W. Shanks, jun., 51 W. Regent-street	
Whitefield - -	Whitefield P., Govan	navy bl and w j, bl k	Alex. M'Intyre, 2 Copeland-rd, Govan	D. M'Intosh, 491 Govan-road, Govan
3rd L.R.V. -	Cathkin Park -	red and black s j -	D. R. Montgomery, 122 S. Portland-st.	W. French, 32 Daisy-st., Govanhill
Do. Strollers	Do.	Do.		T. P. Winter, 12 Warwick-st., S.S.

The fledgling Celtic Football Club was admitted to membership of the SFA in August 1888. Only four of these clubs listed in this SFA Annual of 1888/89 still play football in Glasgow: Celtic, Partick Thistle, Queen's Park and Rangers. Clyde FC is now based in Cumbernauld and Third Lanark went out of existence in 1967, while Shettleston, for example, now play in the Junior grade.

One view of the Celtic vs Third Lanark Scottish Cup Final at (Second) Hampden Park. The match was played in wintry conditions under protest and was dubbed 'The Snow Final'. The strong and established Third Lanark side defeated Celtic, completing their first season in existence, by 3-0 and later won the replay by 2-1. The full name of Celtic's opponents was 3rd Lanark Rifle Volunteers and they were affiliated to a military regiment. (Second) Hampden Park was later owned by the Thirds and re-named Cathkin Park.

Tom Maley, a member of the first Celtic side in the match against Rangers in May 1888. Tom, a schoolmaster, played regularly and later became a noted member of Celtic committees, in which capacity, unlike his brother Willie, he questioned the motion allowing Celtic to become a limited liability company.

A profile of Celtic F C in the 1891/92 edition of a Scottish Football League publication. Celtic had played a leading role in the creation of the League in 1890, the club's open dependence on the paid player being crucial in exposing the 'shamateurism' practised by most clubs in Scotland.

Celtic Football Club.

J. M. NELIS. HON. PRES.

IN last year's publication, we briefly sketched the history of this club up to the opening match in the League Competition, in which they unexpectedly suffered defeat at the hands, or rather the feet, of the famous Renton, a club which, although once renowned as the champions of the world, at that time were not considered in any degree able for such a task as chastising the Parkhead combination, which boasts the possession of some of the finest players in Scotland, and which, in the International match with England of 1889-90, had no fewer than four players. This defeat was followed up with another misfortune to the "Bould Celts," they having been penalised four points for playing ineligible men, and thus was lessened their chance of carrying off the title of champions, for which they yearned, and on which every member of the club had set his heart. These losses, however, only moved the team to greater exertions in the Cup ties, and in the first round for the Scottish Cup they beat the Rangers by one goal to "love," and qualified for the further rounds of the competition. This was a magnificent performance, for the Rangers, having a thoroughly re-organised team, were considered likely lifters of the trophy, and their defeat by the Celts came as a surprise to the entire football community. From this onward,

however, the Celtic seemed to gain courage, and in every game for a considerable time they added fresh laurels, and ultimately ran up to the sixth round of the competition, when they were defeated by Dumbarton, at Boghead, by 3 goals to nil, on a ground from which about four inches of snow had been swept just immediately before the game commenced. Both teams protested against the tie being played, Dumbarton withdrawing theirs, however, but on appeal to the Scottish Committee the Celtic protest was lost by the casting vote of the chairman, Mr. Park, who was present at Boghead when the match was played, and who had previously voted against the Celtic before giving his casting vote. In the competition for the Glasgow Cup, however, the Celtic were more successful, for they beat every club that came before them in the competition, and ran out winners of the trophy, beating the 3rd Lanark in the final by four goals to nil, although the famous Volunteers had previously defeated the Queen's Park in the competition, and were hot favourites.

Being so much taken up with first-class matches, and to an extent behind in their League fixtures, the Celts were very reluctantly compelled to withdraw from the North-Eastern Cup competition, thus giving away the custody of a trophy which they held for the two previous years, and which in

J. GLASS. PRES.

W. M'KILLOP, V.-P.

all probability would have remained on President Glass's sideboard had they continued in the competition. In addition to cup ties, a number of important friendly matches were engaged in during the season—the principal events, as in the past, being with crack English teams. In these the Celtic drew with Sunderland, Blackburn Rovers (English Cup-holders), and Bolton Wanderers, and on other occasions vanquished the two latter teams, in addition to Ardwick, Sheffield Wednesday, and Preston North End.

The club, although standing third in the League competition, occupy the unique distinction of being the only one undefeated by either of the joint-champions—Dumbarton or Rangers—while both these clubs have succumbed to the prowess of the Parkhead team during the course of the competition.

The record of the Celtic for the past season is—Matches played 49, won 34, lost 8, drawn 7 ; scored 148 goals, lost 63—certainly a very good record indeed, and the best the club ever had. From a financial standpoint, the season has been equally prosperous. At the commencement the amount in the hands of the treasurer, Mr. M'Laughlin, was £302 15s. 3d. From members and season ticket-holders the sum drawn was £95 7s. 6d. ; from first eleven matches, £3,748 5s. 10d. ; second eleven matches, £219 14s. 6d. ; other sources,

£61 8s. 2d.—making a total of £4,427 11s. 3d. On the expenditure side, the club has given £545 14s. towards various charitable objects; marriage presents to the extent of £25 have been given to Messrs. James Kelly and J. Reynolds ; while in half gates to clubs, travelling expenses, and general upkeep the sum of £3,582 1s. 6d. has been expended, leaving a balance on hand of £275 9s. 9d. Of this sum £20 was voted to the evicted tenants of Ireland, at the annual meeting held on 16th June last. The players who brought such a rich harvest to the club are well worthy of praise, as Messrs. Bell, Reynolds, M'Keown, Gallagher, Kelly, W. Maley, Madden, M'Ghee, Dowds, M'Mahon, and Campbell formed the finest combination that ever the Celtic Club put forward to fight their battles. In the coming season the club intend to outshine all their previous achievements. With such a team as they have at their disposal they should have little difficulty in reaching high up on the football ladder. All last year's players are ready for the fray, with the addition of one or two new colts, the principal of which (Duff, Cowlairs), will take charge of the Celtic uprights. Guided by such able legislators as J. Nelis, P. Glass, W. M'Killop, T. and W. Maley, and J. H. M'Laughlin there is no fear but the Celtic Club will maintain its position.

W. MALEY, M.-S.

Celtic FC (before switching to the hooped jerseys). Probably the Celtic side which beat Blackburn Rovers 1-0 at Celtic Park in October 1889. Back row: McLaughlin (Goalkeeper), Middle row, left to right: Madden, Coleman, McKeown, Reynolds, Dowds, Cunningham. Front row: Gallagher, M. Dunbar, J. Kelly, Groves. Several committee men are included: Willie McKillop (extreme left, back row), Tom Maley (wearing hat, third from left in the back row), John Glass, Club President, (middle row, next to Reynolds), John O'Hara, Secretary, (next to Dowds), D. Malloy (next to Cunningham).

Celtic's phenomenal early success (and the support generated by the Irish community in Glasgow and further afield) brought the club prosperity unprecedented in Scottish football, as this report proves. The reference to 'the athletic boycott' was caused by the recent decision of the Scottish Amateur Athletic Association to censure Celtic and expel Rangers because of illegal payments made to encourage star performers to appear at the clubs' Annual Sports - a decision later overturned.

An artist's view of the Celtic Sports. Parry, Kibblewhite and Morton were noted English athletes lured to the event. The other four men depicted are members of the committee: John Glass, the club's president, William McKillop, later an MP, and the Maley brothers. Tom and Willie, players and committee men, were also athletes. Willie, for example, won the 100 yards championship of Scotland in 1896.

Parry   Kibblewhite   Morton

J. Glass   W. Mc Killop

T. E. Maley   W. Maley

SKETCHES AT THE CELTIC SPORTS

H. O'NEIL. VAGABOND C.C.
WINNER OF THE 10 MILES.

F.E. BACON, SALFORD HARRIERS

C.A. BRADLEY HUDDERSFIELD A.C.

T.E. MOSSENGER, SALFORD HARRIERS

GODFREY SHAW LONDON A.C.

A SPILL IN THE 100 YDS

GOW WINS THE 100 YDS FROM BRADLEY.

BACON MAKES A RECORD IN THE ONE MILE HANDICAP.

WHO WILL PACE?

O'NEIL PULLS IN YOUNG.

THE FINISH OF THE 10 MILES.

J.M.H.

AT THE CELTIC SPORTS, *19th August, 1893.*

The Celtic Sports were an important annual event in the British athletic calendar. For some decades until its demise the meet attracted participants from both sides of the Atlantic. Note the cartoonist's rendering of the Irish flag (a golden harp on a green background) which flew above Celtic Park until replaced by the tricolour of the fledgling Irish Free State in the 1920s.

16

Sketch Plan of Celtic's New Ground.

JANEFIELD CEMETERY

ROAD TO CLYDE IRON WORKS

SPACE FOR GRAND STANDS

CYCLING TRACK 3½ LAPS = 1 mile

FOOT RUNNING TRACK 4 LAPS = 1 mile

FOOTBALL PITCH

A B C F E D

SPACE FOR GRAND STANDS

NEWLANDS AVENUE

PAVILION

N. B. RAILY C°

New Celtic Ground

Present Ground of Celtic

Janefield cemetery

London Road

Celtic FC literally crossed the road (Janefield Street) in 1892 to the new ground, the site of the present-day stadium. The design of the stadium was influenced by the club's frequent sports meetings - both cycling and track-and-field. (*Scottish Sport*: 2 October 1891)

Celtic Park (seen from London Road). In the foreground is the controversial Grant Stand, named after James Grant, a Celtic director, whose private investment it was. The glass front offered protection from the elements, but the planners had not made any allowance for condensation which obscured the view. (*Evening Times* : 8 April 1904)

17

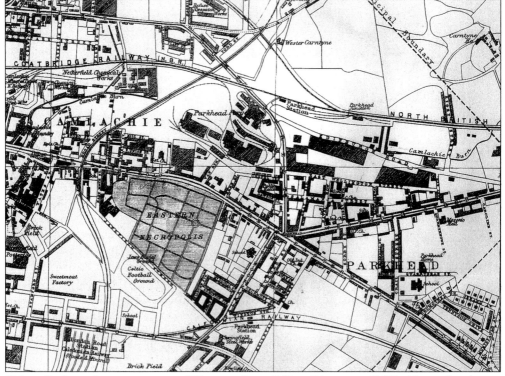

Celtic Park and its environs. (*Glasgow Post Office Directory*: 1907) Note the heavy industrialisation in the area.

(Left) Celtic's 11-0 league victory over Dundee (still a record score for the top Scottish Division) as reported in the inaugural issue of the *Daily Record* (October 28 1895).

(Below) The line-up (from another newspaper).

The attendance at the match was 11,000, the largest ever at a match in Glasgow in which Dundee had been engaged. The "gate" was £284 and the stand drawings £34. The teams were:

Celtic: McArthur; Meechan and Doyle; Maley, Kelly, and Battles; Madden and Blessington; Martin; McMahon and Ferguson.

Dundee: Barrett; Darroch and Burgess; Dundas, Longair, and F. Ferrier, Thomson and Sawers; Vail; McDonald and Keillor.

18

CELTIC
TEAM.

J. CULLEN.

SCOTTISH

1

FACE

AT

J. REYNOLDS.

D. DOYLE.

W. MALEY.

J. KELLY.

P. DOWDS.

A. BRADY.

A. M'MAHON.

N. M'CALLUM.

J. MADDEN.

J. CAMPBELL.

The first Celtic side to win the Scottish Cup. The match against the formidable Queen's Park at Ibrox Park in March 1892 was termed a 'friendly' because of crowd encroachment, but Celtic won the replay by 5-1 on 9 April, having made changes in their line-up. Dowds, a versatile performer, replaced Madden, and Gallagher came in for Dowds. Moustaches, very much in vogue in the late-Victorian era, were considered a sign of manliness. The result could be considered a triumph for professionalism over amateurism and was an indication for the future direction of football in Scotland.

THE BAYARD OF FOOTBALL.

A TRIBUTE TO SANDY M'MAHON. (BY "MAN IN THE KNOW.")

There passed away on Tuesday afternoon the greatest player Association football has ever known. That is not a personal opinion, but it would be the unanimous verdict if a vote were taken of those who were fortunate enough to see the late Alexander M'Mahon—Alexander the Great, I might term him—in the prime of his football career. Fortunately I do not require to labour the point. The spectator of twenty years ago can better tell the story of Sandy's greatness than I or any other writer, even if a whole page of this journal were taken up. I will let the old hands explain to the younger generation what manner of player he was, for it is beyond me to put on record his mystifying gift that amounted to genius. I can only repeat there never was such a wonderful player in all the history of the game, nor are we ever likely to see his equal. He was unique, unapproachable, literally and figuratively, the last word in scientific football, the delight of spectators, the despair of opponents. To analyse his play, to describe his subtle methods, would take up a good deal of space, even if one were able to explain the incomprehensible.

Born in the Border district 45 years ago, Sandy removed to Edinburgh, and when quite a lad attracted the notice of senior clubs by his play in a junior club, the Woodburn. A short term followed at Easter Road, and then he came to Parkhead at the close of 1890. His first match was against Dumbarton on the New Year's Day of 1891, and he had the pleasure of seeing his future partner on the left wing score the equalising goal. But not until the season 1891-2 did

M'Mahon and Campbell

begin that career as the great left-wing of all time. Sandy had come to Parkhead as a centre-forward, and filled this position for nearly three months. About the middle of March the Celts set out on their first Lancashire trip—they had already crossed the Border and met the Corinthians at the Oval in 1889—and it was then that the M'Mahon-Campbell partnership began, to last several seasons, and astonish the football world by its brilliancy. The first match was at Bolton and ended in a draw—2 goals each. Sandy went clean through the Bolton defence to score the equalising goal, and at the finish 2300 spectators waited outside and accompanied him to the hotel, cheering him all the way. Such football they had never thought possible as Sandy showed all through the game. Next day the Celts met Ardwick, won by 7—2, and the left-wing again carried off the honours. Two days later found the boys at Blackburn on top by 2 goals to 0, with M'Mahon fooling Dewar, Barton, and Brandon to such an extent that Geordie Dewar spoke to Campbell on the field and asked him who in thunder was the unknown player who could do as he liked with the mighty Rovers. Then on to Sheffield, to win by 3—1, and home again, tired out but happy, though they had to go down to Paisley at the week-end, where they lost to the Saints in a League match by 1—0, and lost the championship as well. However, if the League Championship was lost, the three cups were won next season, and the championship lost by only 2 points, Dumbarton gaining 37 points to Celts' 35. The season of 1891-2 was the Celts' first great season, and the first in which M'Mahon and Campbell played together from start to finish. Sandy was capped against England that season and was one of the eleven

Associated with the Dreadful Ibrox Disaster.

Next season Scotland claimed both Celtic wingers, and if we were beaten at Richmond the fault lay not with the Celtic contingent — M'Mahon, Campbell, W. Maley, and Kelly. Three times was M'Mahon capped against England, and other international honours were showered upon him, he and Willie Maley also figuring against the Canadians in 1891.

(Continued on Page 5.)

(Continued on Page 5.)

FAMOUS CELT'S DEATH
(Continued from Page 3.)

Unfortunately he had first one knee and then the other put out, to say nothing of an ankle, so that long before his time he had to drop out of the game, leaving behind him a reputation such as no other player is ever likely to gain. Had it not been for the accident that befel him I feel certain he would have beaten Alec. Smith in point of years of service, for his was the style which required neither speed nor virility for success. He could get through a game on one leg, I might say, and that he had to do many a time; indeed, it seems he had hirpled through a Cup Final on Old Cathkin, and helped to beat Rangers. To reprint an old saying, I may add that as a footballer and a gentleman-footballer, we shall never look upon his like again.

On and off the field he was the same good-natured, philosophical, kindly fellow, taking the frowns and smiles of fortune like the man he was. He was as difficult to upset temperamentally as physically, and was never known to grumble. I am betraying no confidence when I state that his last words to the clergyman who attended him on his deathbed were words of gratitude. He thanked the reverend gentleman for all he had done for him, and near the finish, when speech was denied him, he smiled and gently pressed the visitors' hands when told that Willie Maley, Michael Dunbar, Johnnie Campbell, and other old friends, were standing over him. That was Sandy; smiling and grateful, kind and affectionate, facing death without fear, leaving life void of regret. So passed away the Bayard of football, without fear, without reproach—the type of a perfect gentleman.—R.I.P.

The funeral to Dalbeth Cemetery took place on Thursday afternoon from the residence of his brother, Mr James M'Mahon, 28 Slatefield Street, Glasgow. The mourners included:—Messrs T. White, J. Kelly, J.P., J. Colgan, M. Dunbar, J. Shaughnessy, W. Maley, P. M. Rogers, A. Murphy, J. Cruden, etc.

The funeral arrangements were efficiently carried out by Mr F. M'Cabe, 71 London Street, Glasgow.

Sandy McMahon's obituary tribute in the *Glasgow Observer* of 29 January 1916.

Sandy McMahon – 'The Prince of Dribblers', who formed a legendary left-wing partnership with Johnny Campbell.

St Mary's, the first of the Celtic brake clubs, came from the Calton, Celtic's birthplace. The early clubs travelled to the matches in style with trumpets blaring on four-in-hand wagons decorated in bunting, and often displaying the club banner depicting a favourite player. The brake clubs were attached to the parish's League of the Cross, a Catholic temperance organisation.

Advertisement for a social evening.

GLASGOW OBSERVER, SATURDAY, JANUARY 18, 1896

ANNUAL FESTIVAL OF THE UNITED

"CELTIC" BRAKE CLUBS
AND FRIENDS,
WILL BE HELD IN THE

GRAND NATIONAL HALLS,
MAIN STREET, S.S.,
On FRIDAY EVENING, 31st Jan., 1896.

JOHN GLASS, Esq., President Celtic F.C., in the Chair.

The following Talented Artistes will appear—
MISS MALONE,
Distinguished Scottish Contralto;
MR R. GALLOUGHER,
Favourite Tenor;
MR TOM MILNER,
Scotland's Favourite Comedian.
MR J. A. WILSON,
Eccentric Negro Comedian and Dancer.
Mr C. BURNE, Pianist.
Mr J. HUTCHEON............Purveyor.

Doors open at Seven o'clock; Tea on the Table at Half-past Seven prompt.
Adult's Ticket, 1s 6d.; Juvenile's Ticket, 1s.

An Assembly will take place immediately after the Concert, for which Mr C. Burne's Celebrated Quadrille Band has been engaged. Mr A. J. Tierney, M.C., Ticket (admitting Lady and Gent.), 2s 6d. No Gentleman admitted unless accompanied by a Lady. Spectators' Tickets, 6d each.

Tickets to be had from the following Gentlemen :—Mr M'Gill, President, 27 Charlotte Street; Mr Malone, 20 Shamrock Street, S.S.; Mr Ward, Treasurer, 36 Commerce Street, S.S.; Mr J. Moore, Secretary, 72 William Street, Anderston; also at St Mary's, St John's, St Francis', and St Patrick's League of the Cross Halls.

Before the days of action photographs, newspapers had to rely on drawings and cartoons to capture the flavour of football matches. This cartoon is from the Glasgow-based magazine *The Bailie* of October in 1898 after Rangers and Celtic had met in the Glasgow Cup, a match which ended in a 1-1 draw.

Celtic Park, recognised as one of the best stadiums in Britain by the turn of the century, hosted the lucrative Scotland vs England international match five times between 1894 and 1904. In the 1900 fixture, won 4-1 by Scotland, Lord Rosebery attended and the Scottish side wore hooped jerseys of pink and primrose, his racing colours. Reputedly, the nobleman had offered the Scottish players 'one pound a man' to beat England.

Rangers' disappointment at losing the Scottish Cup Final to Celtic after being two goals up early in the contest. Jimmy Quinn established his status as a Celtic folk-hero by scoring all three goals in a thrilling comeback. (*Scottish Referee*: 18 April 1904)

Jimmy Quinn, regarded by many as the greatest Celtic centre forward of them all. Colm Brogan, the broadcaster, described him as an athlete 'whose name lives long after he has ceased to perform. Such a man was James Quinn. There was nobody quite like him before his time, there has been nobody like him since.'

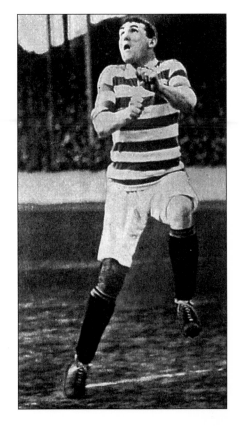

Quinn is depicted both as a youth shortly after joining Celtic in 1901 and at the height of his powers a decade later. Quinn died in November 1945 and Brogan added that 'his endless zeal kept the supporters of the opposing team always uneasy and the Celtic supporters always hopeful. No game was ever lost until Quinn had left the field.'

Jimmy Quinn in the wars. The great centre forward is being led off for treatment, probably while playing for Scotland in the Rosebery colours. One journalist described the Scottish forward line on one occasion as 'Jimmy Quinn, all Quinn, and nothing but Quinn'.

A *Scottish Referee* cartoon of 6 January 1905 suggests the tightness of the race for the championship as the Old Firm began their domination of Scottish football. Celtic became champions after winning a play-off match 2-1, refereed by an English official at Hampden Park in May. Both Rangers and Celtic had finished level on points and neither goal average nor goal difference was used then to decide the outcome. This win started off Celtic's historic run of six titles in a row.

John Madden (Glasgow Rangers),
trainer S. K. Slavia.

Two dapper Celts, Johnny Madden and Willie Orr. Madden, a centre forward in Celtic's early days, went to coach in Czechoslovakia from 1905 to 1938 where he imported the traditional Scottish short-passing style. He was a martinet, latterly supervising the training sessions from his wheelchair while reputedly brandishing a cabbie's whip to get the message across. The card depicting Madden was a publicity handout from Slavia Prague - who confused the members of the Old Firm.

Willie Orr was more genial, although a stalwart, and a no-nonsense defender who played during the first decade of this century. He also went into management and guided the unfashionable Airdrieonians to victory over Hibernian in the 1924 Scottish Cup Final.

The nucleus of the squad that carved out Celtic's first great era, characterised most notably by winning the league championship six times in a row (1905 to 1910). Note that the goalkeeper (Davie Adams) could be distinguished from the outfield players only by his cap. Back row, left to right: R.Davis (Trainer), Campbell, McLeod, Watson, .Hamilton (A.), McNair, Wilson, Garry, McCourt, Adams. Front row: Young, Hay, Bennett, McMenemy, Loney, Quinn, Somers, McNair(W.). During the historic run, surpassed by Jock Stein's side of 1972, their league record was as follows: P 192 W136 L23 D33 F444 A153 PTS 306.

Willie Loney, one of a long list of notable Celtic centre halves, is featured in this *Glasgow Observer* portrait of 19 March 1910. The redoubtable Loney was nicknamed 'The Obliterator.'

A cameo of the versatile Alec McNair, described by the *Scottish Weekly Record* in August 1915 as 'a genius in offence and defence... Nothing is more remarkable than the calm way in which he lets an opponent scheme and plan - and then robs him at the crucial moment'. This portrait of 'The Icicle' appeared in the 7 May 1910 edition of the *Glasgow Observer*.

A *Glasgow Observer* (30 April 1910) portrait of Celtic goalkeeper Davie Adams. The newspaper added that Adams 'complains that behind such good backs as he has, he gets cold doing nothing.'

Frequently, 'friendly matches' were arranged against English sides. In April 1912 Aston Villa visited Celtic Park and fought out a 1-1 draw. In this goalmouth incident keeper John Mulrooney punches clear as 'Sunny Jim' Young lends support.

In the same match against Aston Villa the famous Celtic full-back partnership of Alec McNair (left) and Joe Dodds watch anxiously while the well-dressed referee awaits developments.

Celtic's outside right Andy McAtee jousts with a Queen's Park defender at Hampden Park in May 1917. By winning 1-0 Celtic established a record of six successive Glasgow Charity Cup Final victories.

Patsy Gallacher at his tricks in a 1912 match. Jimmy Quinn hovers in the background, and Patsy's 'victim' is believed to be Bob Mercer of Hearts. One journalist described the frail-looking Gallacher as 'the ghost with the magic feet but Willie Maley, on the other hand, pointed out that 'Gallacher played for two decades in first-class football without showing any trace of wear and tear.' He added: 'There were players who resolved to stop Gallacher (by any means). Did they succeed? Not on your life!'

THE CELTIC FOOTBALL CLUB.

A NOTABLE COMBINATION.

Anxious to do a little for local charities, some East-end gentlemen induced Hibernians and Renton to play a benefit match at Barrowfield Park, Bridgeton, for a handsome trophy, in 1886. A considerable sum was thus obtained, and this set the promoters thinking: Why not form a football club composed of young Irish players and let the gate-drawings, minus expenses, go to local Catholic charities? It was one thing to hold meetings and draw up rules, but an entirely different matter to attract the right class of player to the new club. Every effort was made to induce some of the Hibernian players to come to Parkhead, but they were reluctant to leave Easter Road, and there was every prospect of the scheme being dropped when the late Mr. Glass induced Mr. James Kelly to lend a helping hand. Once Mr. Kelly gave his consent the other players followed suit, and soon there was a powerful eleven built up from the Hibernian, Renton, Third Lanark, and Cowlairs clubs. A few friendly matches were played in the months of May and June, 1888, and in August the Celts opened their first season, and what a successful first season was that of 1888-9, the club running into the final of the Scottish Cup, and ultimately losing to the Third Lanark. The history of the club is closely identified with the history of Scottish football; the club has maintained a leading place in both League and Cup competitions, and has furnished many International players.

Though several claim the honour of founding the Celtic Club, none deny that, but for the adherence of Mr. James Kelly, such players as Groves, M'Callum, Maley, Dunlop, and Gallacher, would not have joined the new venture. Mr. Kelly had already gained an International reputation, both as a forward and a half-back, and it was his personality which laid the foundation of the club's success. The highest honours fell to the fastest centre half-back that Scotland

Mr. James Kelly, J.P.

has produced, and he was capped against England five times, against the English League four times, against Ireland thrice, against the Irish League three times, and once against Wales.

Mr. Kelly settled in Blantyre some years ago and is a county J.P., a member of the local School Board, and president of Celtic Football Club.

James Quinn, the Celtic and International centre-forward, and an outstanding personality in Scottish football, was born at Smithston, Dumbartonshire. His play as a junior in the village team led to his being, in January, 1901, signed on for Celtic F. C. His first position in the team was that of outside-left, but his dashing style won for him the more responsible position of centre-forward. Since then, the Celtic team has carried all before it, winning every trophy and establishing records which will probably never be surpassed.

Standing about 5 ft. 8½ ins. and weighing over 12 st., Quinn is a stumbling-block to the most resolute centre-halves, and as a shot is dreaded by all goal-keepers. He eschews the more polished methods of such as R. S. M'Coll and G. O. Smith, confident in his strength and dash. Of his achievements Quinn cannot be got to speak, but is ever ready with advice and encouragement for a young player. The team's Continental tour gave him a European reputation, his play being the chief attraction. The football exploits of Quinn will long be talked of.

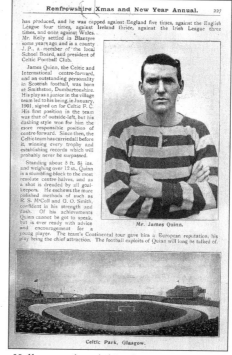

Mr. James Quinn.

Celtic Park, Glasgow.

From the 1911/12 edition of this annual. James Kelly was the club's chairman at the time, following a successful career as Celtic's first captain and star player, while Jimmy Quinn was nearing the end of a remarkable career.

Willie Angus, a Victoria Cross winner who had been on Celtic's books, was given a rousing reception when he was invited to attend a Glasgow Cup tie at Parkhead in September 1915. He had earned his VC in France by crossing 'No Man's Land' to rescue a wounded officer. He suffered forty wounds, including the loss of an eye, and was invalided out of the army. James Kelly supports Angus in his walk around the track, accompanied by Willie Maley. Two other Celtic players, Peter Johnstone and Frank Kelly (James Kelly's eldest son), would lose their lives while on service in France.

Two
1918-1945

Patsy Gallacher, wearing an international 'cap'. Born in Donegal in 1893, Gallacher was eligible to play for Eire and Northern Ireland and he won representative honours with both.

"PATSY"—by Alan Morton

WITHIN 20 yards of goal Patsy Gallacher was the most dangerous forward I have ever seen. You never knew what he would do. Often he would wriggle through, past man after man, with defenders reluctant to tackle in case they gave away a penalty kick.

I played alongside him once, and on another occasion we were in the same team. He was my partner in a Glasgow-Sheffield game at Hampden, and when I think of that game I wonder why it is that International players in these days go away before a game to get to know each other better. Patsy and I dovetailed at once, as I think all real International players ought to be able to do.

After a bit he said to me:—" Let's kid them on." We did a bit of kidding, and I remember the Sheffield right half towards the end of the game saying to his right back:—" Come on there, get after them ! " and the right back replying:—" You can chase them if you like, but I've had enough —— running around for the day ! "

Patsy was transferred to the Rangers to play in Andy Cunningham's benefit match but he did not play alongside me that night. He was at inside right to Sandy Archibald. He was in the Falkirk team which beat us at Ibrox (in the Scottish Cup) after a draw at Brockville, and, of course, he played in many games for Celtic against Rangers.

Our fellows used to say after one of those " Old Firm " games :—" There's Patsy off scot-free and we're sore all over."

He was an astonishing little man, and I could not agree with those who thought he played more than the ball. He was so quick on his feet that impression may have been easy to acquire, but I could not see it that way.

In summing up a position and in taking the responsibility for getting a goal himself Patsy was absolutely unsurpassed in my time. . . .

They called him the " Mighty Atom " and they called him a freak. He was simply a great natural player whose unbounded skill as a ball-player cast all physical drawbacks aside.

There never was a player like him, and I often wonder if we shall see his like again. I wish we could, just to show the present-day players that we of Patsy Gallacher's time had something to boast about.

A tribute to Patsy by Alan Morton of Rangers, written after Gallacher's death in 1953 and reproduced in the *Celtic View* of 15 March 1967. Morton, a contemporary of Gallacher, is still generally considered the greatest Rangers' winger.

Some Celtic supporters still consider Patsy Gallacher 'the greatest player of them all', recalling his equalising goal against Dundee in the 1925 Scottish Cup Final as the most unique goal ever scored. Gallacher reportedly dribbled past several defenders in a crowded goalmouth and ended up by somersaulting into the net with the ball lodged between his feet.

Celtic in 1919/20. Back row, left to right: Gallacher, Cringan, Gilchrist, McAtee, McCall, Cassidy, McNair, Pratt, Watson, Craig, Livingstone. Front row: McMenemy, McLean, Shaw, Brown, McInally. The two players between Cassidy (back row, fifth from left) and McAtee (eighth from left) have not been identified clearly and, thus, have not been named.

Patsy Gallacher in a contemplative mood.

Celtic FC in 1922/23. Back row, left to right: Hilley, McStay (W.), Gallacher, Gilchrist, J.B. Murphy. Middle row: W. Quinn (Trainer), McMaster, McNair, McFarlane, Glasgow, McLean, Cringan. Front row: McAtee, McStay (J.), J.F. Murphy, Shaw, Cassidy, Crilley, Connolly.

The Old Firm captains Willie McStay (Celtic) and Alan Morton (Rangers) pictured before the traditional Ne'erday derby in 1927 at Ibrox with the referee, Mr T. Small (Dundee).

Rangers' keeper Tom Hamilton was caught by surprise in the early minutes of the match when Alec Thomson scored for Celtic.

Adam McLean, Eddie McGarvey (Trainer) and Willie McStay enjoy a break while training at Seamill. McLean was an exceptional winger and unfortunate to be a contemporary of Alan Morton. He established a good understanding with Jimmy McGrory and laid on many goals for the centre forward. McStay was a sound full-back who provided leadership on the field as Celtic's captain in the 1920s.

Celtic players relax on the links at Dunbar while training for the 1927 Scottish Cup Final against East Fife. From left to right: Tommy McInally, Adam McLean and trainer Eddie McGarvie (wearing the chain) watch John ('Jean') McFarlane drive off.

Tommy McInally in action during the 1927 Scottish Cup Final against East Fife, won 3-1 by Celtic. Tommy was treated like the 'Prodigal Son' by manager Willie Maley, who indulged the player's waywardness with a generosity rarely extended to McInally's team-mates. According to one account, Maley challenged McInally about having been seen outside a public house late on the eve of a match only to be met with the response: 'Aye, Boss, that's right. Ah hid tae leave the place - it was closing time.'

Tommy McInally practises his overhead kicking in this 1925 match at Celtic Park. Note the old pavilion, destroyed by fire in March 1929.

Celtic and Hearts pictured before the kick-off on the first day of the 1929/30 season - when the new stand was opened at Celtic Park. Celtic players, Back row, left to right: Thomson (A.), McGonagle, Thomson (J.), Scarff, Geatons. Front row: Connolly, McStay (J.), Kavanagh McGrory, Wilson. The Hearts' goalkeeper is Jack Harkness, Thomson's rival for Scottish 'caps' and later a distinguished journalist with the Sunday Post. Behind the teams is the famed covered enclosure later known as 'The Jungle'. The new stand replaced the recently demolished 'Grant Stand' and could accommodate 4,800 spectators.

Jimmy McGrory, John Thomson and Willie Maley (seated) with Brother Dunstan, the headmaster of St Joseph's College, Dumfries, c. 1930. Brother Walfrid, one of Celtic's founders, is buried in the grounds of the Marist College.

Jimmy McGrory, famed for his heading ability, poses for the studio camera. No player has ever scored so many goals in the top flight of British football as Jimmy McGrory. A team-mate, reflecting on the club's indebtedness to McGrory's goalscoring and commitment, stated: 'Jimmy McGrory was Celtic!'

Celtic FC in 1930. Back row, left to right: Cook, Kavanagh, Smith, Wilson. Middle row: McGonagle, Geatons, O'Hare, Thomson (J.), Whitelaw, Hughes, W. Quinn (Trainer). Front row: Thomson (R.), Thomson (A.), McGrory, McStay (J.), Scarff, Napier.

Jimmy McGrory heads a goal past Scottish internationalist Johnny Jackson in the Scottish Cup against Partick Thistle at Parkhead in February 1933. Celtic won 2-1 and later defeated Motherwell 1-0 in the Final at Hampden. Inevitably, the scorer in that final was McGrory.

A sequence illustrating Jimmy McGrory's goal in the 1931 Scottish Cup Final against Motherwell. Celtic trailed by 0-2 with only seven minutes left but fought back to equalise in the dying seconds. Jimmy McGrory lunged at a Napier free kick for the first goal and inspired the dramatic comeback. (Below) McGrory stumbles forward after contact with the ball as keeper McClory watches helplessly.

A group of Celtic players enjoying a break from training at Celtic Park in 1931. Back row, left to right: Willie Cook, William 'Peter' McGonagle, John Thomson. Middle row: Chic Geatons, Peter Scarff, Peter Wilson, Alec Thomson. Front row: Jimmy McGrory, Charlie Napier, Jimmy McStay (Captain), Bertie Thomson .

A section of the crowd at the 1931 Scottish Cup Final. Taken in front of the stand at Hampden Park, the photograph suggests that football's appeal was not confined to the working class.

INTERNATIONAL SOCCER

The World Famous

GLASGOW CELTIC

vs.

PAWTUCKET RANGERS

SOUVENIR PROGRAM

Providence Cycledrome

SATURDAY, JUNE 6, 1931

A Celtic vs Rangers match, but in Providence, Rhode Island. The 'friendly' turned into a roughhouse affair and Celtic required a police escort at time-up. Willie Maley was far from complimentary about the arrangements: 'The ground was like a furnace, the dressing-room conditions disgraceful and the referee had no control whatever.'

Peter Scarff and Bertie Thomson during the club's tour of North America in 1931. Tragedy was to strike them soon as both these players were to die within a few years, Peter of tuberculosis and Bertie of heart trouble.

Celtic's captain Jimmy McStay poses with the Scottish Cup with the Mayor of Philadelphia prior to the opening match of the American tour in May 1931. Celtic won this match by 6-1 against the Pennsylvania All-Stars.

By 1931 Celtic's young goalkeeper John Thomson was the best in the country. Although still in his early twenties, Thomson had already won four caps for Scotland. Shortly after halftime in the Old Firm fixture at Ibrox on 5 September, Thomson made a typically brave clearance at the feet of Rangers' centre forward, Sam English, but suffered a serious head injury. He died later that night in the Victoria Infirmary. (Above) Players begin to gather around John Thomson. From the reactions of the Celtic defenders nobody blames Sam English for the clash.

Celtic players call for the ambulance men as their trainer works on John Thomson. English ignores his own trainer in his anxiety over Thomson's injury.

Chic Geatons takes over from Thomson in Celtic's goal. McStay, Napier, Thomson (R.) and Thomson (A.) offer silent encouragement.

Jimmy McGrory in action against Queen's Park's Bob Gillespie at Celtic Park. Both sides wore black armbands in honour of John Thomson, Celtic's goalkeeper, who had died the previous Saturday. The match, played in a subdued manner, ended in a 2-2 draw.

John Thomson's parents stand before a photograph of their son at a miners' hall in Bowhill, Fife.

'Peter' McGonagle, a dedicated Celt, leads out the team. Joe Kennaway is next in line.

Joe Kennaway was the man chosen by Maley to succeed John Thomson. Kennaway had impressed the manager during the 1931 tour of America when he inspired his Fall River side to a 1-0 win over the tourists. He proved a reliable replacement for Thomson.

Celtic reserve teams were the breeding ground for the players (such as Jimmy Delaney, Malcolm MacDonald and Johnny Crum) who brought the club success in the late 1930s. Astonishingly, Celtic had dispensed with a reserve side in 1922 to save money and paid a heavy price until reversing the decision in 1930.

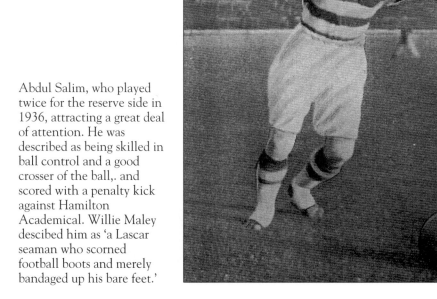

Abdul Salim, who played twice for the reserve side in 1936, attracting a great deal of attention. He was described as being skilled in ball control and a good crosser of the ball,. and scored with a penalty kick against Hamilton Academical. Willie Maley descibed him as 'a Lascar seaman who scorned football boots and merely bandaged up his bare feet.'

Four legendary Celts at Parkhead prior to Jimmy McGrory's testimonial match against Rangers in August 1934. From left to right: Jimmy Quinn, Willie Maley (then Celtic's manager), Jimmy McGrory and Patsy Gallacher, who acted as a linesman.

McGrory, Quinn and Alan Morton at the same match.

Celtic at the pre-season public trial in 1933/34. Back row, from left to right: Thomson (R.), Kennedy, Paterson, Divers, Connor. Middle row: Dunn, Wallace, MacDonald, Boyle, Kennaway, Morrison, McGonagle, Smith, Buchan, O'Donnell (F.), Quskley (J.) (Trainer), Thomson (A.). Front row: Wilson, Crum, McGrory, Dawson, McStay (J.), Hughes, Hogg, O'Donnell (H.), Napier.

Jimmy McGrory scored 410 league goals (397 with Celtic and 13 for Clydebank), but not this time as he is foiled by Hibernian's goalkeeper.

In April 1933 a Hearts/Hibernian Select played a Celtic/Rangers Select at Tynecastle with the proceeds going to the Granton Trawler Disaster Fund. The Glasgow side wore Celtic jerseys. Back Row, from left to right: - McPhail (Rangers), Kennaway (Celtic), Archibald, Fleming and Gray (all Rangers), Geatons (Celtic). Front row: - Brown (Rangers, sitting on the ground), Thomson, McStay, McGrory and McGonagle (all Celtic).

A balletic scene at Ibrox Park in September 1935, involving Rangers' pivot Jimmy Simpson and Celtic's centre forward Johnny Crum, who scored in a 2-1 victory, the visitors' first league win there since January 1921.

The O'Donnell brothers, Hugh and Frank. Celtic have had several other pairs of brothers representing them. Among them, Tom and Willie Maley, Jimmy and Willie McStay, John and Billy McPhail, Frank and Jim Brogan, and Paul and Willie McStay.

Willie Buchan and Johnny Crum, the goalscorers in the 1937 Scottish Cup Final against Aberdeen, display the trophy inside a deserted Hampden Park. An hour or so earlier a record crowd for a club match in Europe (146,433) had watched Celtic win by 2-1.

Malcolm MacDonald takes the training at Celtic Park in the mid-1930s. Among the starters are Matt Lynch (third from left), Alex Millar (fifth) and John Divers (sixth).

Celtic's Empire Exhibition Trophy side, considered by some as the equal of the 1967 Lisbon Lions. Back row, from left to right: Geatons, Hogg, Kennaway, Morrison, Crum, Paterson. Front row: Delaney, MacDonald, Lyon, Divers, Murphy.

Jimmy Delaney challenges Sunderland's goalkeeper in the opening match of the Empire Exhibition Tournament while Divers and Murphy look on.

Johnny Crum succeeded the great McGrory as Celtic's centre forward and scored the winning goal at Ibrox Park in the Empire Exhibition Final against Everton in 1938. Intelligent interchanging with the other members of a famous forward line was a feature of his game.

BRITISH EMPIRE
EXHIBITION TROPHY
1938

First Round

*Celtic	0	Sunderland	0
Celtic	3	Sunderland	1
Aberdeen	4	Chelsea	0
Everton	2	Rangers	0
Hearts	1	Brentford	0

Semi-Final

Celtic	1	Hearts	0
Everton	3	Aberdeen	2

Final

*Celtic	1	Everton	0

*After extra time

Scorers

Celtic—Crum 3, Divers 2 Everton—Lawton 2, Boyes, Cunliffe, Cooper (Aberdeen) own goal. Aberdeen—Armstrong 2 Strauss 2, Thomson, Hamilton. Hearts—Briscoe. Sunderland—Saunders.

41

From the Celtic Football Guide of 1938/39.

Willie Lyon receives the Empire Exhibition Trophy from the Earl of Elgin. Waiting for their momentoes are Kennaway and Geatons.

Celtic receive the Charity Cup at Glasgow City Chambers. Until a decade or so after the Second World War, both the Glasgow Cup and the Charity Cup were highly-regarded competitions, but they declined rapidly with an expanded schedule and European competition. The players in the background include Morrison, Murphy, Paterson, Hogg, Lyon (with trophy), Delaney and Buchan. On the extreme left is Willie Maley, on the right is Tom White (Chairman) and behind him is Bob Kelly, his successor.

Three
1945-1965

Willie Fernie, a star of the 1950s, dribbles past an East Fife defender at Methil.

55 Walter St.,
Glasgow. E.1
22/6/46.

Dear Matt,

In certain circles my writing to you would have the same effect as a bomb exploding, but I felt that, if we are to live up to the name of sport, then I must say something. I knew, like many others, that two Celtic players had to appear before the S.F.A. for being ordered off the field, but no one was more surprised than I when, on the morning after the S.F.A.

meeting, I read in the papers that you had been suspended for a month. As you may well know, I had been asked by dozens of persons for my impression of the "scene." Believe me Matt, not once in all my explanations to these people did I have to incriminate you as an instigator, with the result that when they asked me why you had been suspended I just had no answer for them. If my memory serves me right and I am sure it does, when the referee gave his decision he was immediately surrounded

by Celtic players. It was then, and about this I am positive, you came walking over to me and said "I don't want to get mixed up in any trouble here, Jimmy, I have been in enough of that." It was then that I said to you to try and get the Celtic players who were still protesting to keep their heads cool. You then walked back to the penalty area and appeared to me to be doing just that. You can imagine my surprise then, Matt, when I read you had been suspended for a month. I thought perhaps you would

have appealed, but so far I have seen no word of it.

I remember someone discussing the game afterwards, asking me how the players of both teams were conducting themselves prior to the penalty incident, my reply was that I thought it was one of the best Old Firm games for some time and that if I always got as clean a game as I get from Matt Lynch then it would be a pleasure to play every Saturday. In closing let me wish you every success in the new season.

Yours in sport,
Jimmy Duncanson.

In the Victory Cup (1946) two Celtic players were ordered off for disputing the award of a penalty kick to Rangers in the Semi-final replay, lost by 2-0. They (Paterson and Mallan) were later suspended for three months by the SFA. A third Celt (Matt Lynch - who had not been ordered off nor cautioned) was also suspended for a month. Mystified, Lynch attempted to appeal and contacted Jimmy Duncanson, his immediate opponent. Duncanson's letter, which reflects credit on both players, is re-produced in full. Despite the evidence, Lynch was obliged to serve his suspension 'for inciting his team to leave the field'.

Ronnie Simpson (left) in the jersey of Queen's Park for whom he made his debut in 1945 at the age of 14! In 1964 he would sign for Celtic from Hibernian and continue playing until 1969.

Celtic prepare to board the train for Aberdeen in the late 1940s. Back row, left to right: Mallan, McMillan, Kiernan, Miller, Hogg, Lynch, Milne, Corbett, Gallacher (W.). Prominent in the front row are Joe Rae and Bobby Evans.

Crowds, desperate for entertainment after the Second World War, flocked to the grounds in the late 1940s. This was the scene outside Dens Park in January 1947 for Celtic's Scottish Cup tie with Dundee.

Another view of the crowd outside Dens Park.

Bobby Hogg leads out Celtic for the Dens cup-tie, followed by Miller, Mallan, Kiernan, Rae and Evans.

Willie Miller clears as Willie Corbett and Matt Lynch watch, but Celtic went down 2-1 to their opponents from the 'B' Division. Throughout the Second World War the Celtic administration had allowed the club to wither drastically. It would be some seasons before the club fielded a side worthy of its great traditions.

In the same match, Lynch (Dundee) saves as Gerry McAloon, Joe Rae and Bobby Evans wait hopefully.

Willie Miller watches a Dundee shot balloon over the bar with Willie Corbett in attendance.

On 17 April 1948, the last regular day of the season, Celtic travelled to Dens Park knowing that only a victory there would ensure Division 'A' status. Patsy Gallacher's sons, Tommy (Dundee) and Willie (Celtic), playing in direct opposition, were watched by their father as Celtic recorded a 3-2 win.

An idol of the Celtic Park terracings - Charlie Tully. The Irishman had been bought from Belfast Celtic in 1948 in an attempt to arrest the decline into mediocrity - or worse. His skills and personality quickly made him the most talked-about footballer in the country.

One of the greatest wing halves in Celtic's history - Bobby Evans. The red-headed Evans was a bundle of energy and enthusiasm, unfortunately too often in losing causes until the 1950s.

Willie Miller kicks clear from Billy Williamson of Rangers at Ibrox in September 1949. This match, won 4-0 by Rangers, was partially boycotted by Celtic supporters in a protest at the perceived unjust refereeing in two previous Old Firm matches that season, most notably the infamous 'Cox-Tully incident' in a League Cup tie. Only 65,000 saw the league fixture in contrast to the 95,000 who had attended the League Cup match; Cox is the other Rangers player in the photograph.

Lazio and Celtic line up
before the start of a 'friendly'
in Rome in May 1950, held
to celebrate the Italian club's
jubilee. The match ended 0-0
and Celtic's captain John
McPhail was ordered off
along with a Lazio defender.
A 'rematch' in Glasgow a few
months later ended in a 4-0
win for Celtic with McPhail
scoring all the goals. Celtic
players, from left to right are:
McPhail, Bonnar, Baillie,
Tully, Fernie, Evans,
McGrory, Haughney,
Peacock, Collins, Milne,
Mallan, Fallon.

John McPhail exchanges gifts
with Lazio's captain.

John McPhail lofts the ball over Motherwell's Johnstone to win the 1951 Scottish Cup for Celtic. Shaw and Paton are helpless onlookers.

Further action from the 1951 Final. Bertie Peacock challenges Motherwell's keeper while Weir and McPhail watch, as do the crowd of 131,393 at Hampden Park.

Success at last! Tully hugs McPhail as referee J. Mowat blows for time-up. It was Celtic's first major success since the Empire Exhibition Trophy in 1938.

John McPhail borne aloft by Alec Boden and Sean Fallon after the 1951 Scottish Cup Final.

Club colours had become much more in evidence on the terracing by the early 1950s.

St Peter's Celtic Supporters' Club, Belfast, on a visit to Glasgow for the Old Firm fixture in September 1951. Only two years earlier Belfast Celtic - named after their Glasgow counterparts - had disbanded following disturbances during and after a match with Linfield.

A proud Celtic squad display the Scottish Cup on board the *Queen Mary* as they travel to the United States. Trainer Alec Dowdells holds the trophy.

Bertie Peacock challenges during the club's tour of North America in the summer of 1951, with Bobby Collins in attendance. The markings on the pitch and the bleacher seats suggest the match was played in a baseball stadium.

After the 1951 tour Celtic posed with some of their souvenirs. Back row, left to right: Desmond White (Secretary), Evans, Fernie, Rollo, Boden, Hunter, Baillie, Mallan, Bob Kelly (Chairman), McGrory, Tom Devlin (Director). Front row: Alec Dowdells (Trainer), Millsopp, Fallon, Weir, Collins, McPhail, Peacock, Milne, Tully, Jimmy McGrory (Manager).

Celtic's makeshift side, with two full-backs in the forward line, beat Rangers by 2-1 in September 1952. Alec Rollo, selected at outside right, scored the second goal with this speculative lob. The black armbands were in honour of John Millsopp, a young Celtic player who had died earlier that week. Players from both sides had attended the funeral on the day of the match but the minute's silence at Celtic Park was sadly interrupted by some Rangers supporters.

How the *Scottish Daily Mail* cartoonist saw the 1953 Charity Cup Final, won 3-1 by Celtic. Featured prominently is Neil Mochan, signed the day before from Middlesbrough. Mochan went on to play in the Coronation Cup and led Celtic to an unexpected triumph in the matches against Arsenal, Manchester United and Hibernian. Mochan played his first four matches for Celtic at Hampden Park and picked up two medals before appearing in Celtic colours at Celtic Park.

Neil Mochan's goal in the Coronation Cup Final against Hibernian in 1953 would be long remebered. From more than thirty yards his ferocious shot beat Tommy Younger, one of Scotland's best goalkeepers, to give Celtic a 1-0 lead.

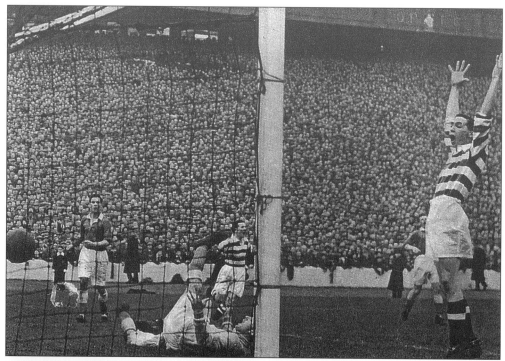

John Higgins, a skilful right-winger whose career would be curtailed by knee injuries, jumps for joy as Mochan's shot is deflected past Martin by Aberdeen's pivot, Young, in the 1954 Scottish Cup Final. Mochan, who finished the season as Celtic's top scorer, usually played at centre forward but could be used effectively as a left-winger where his forte was a viciously swerving cross-shot.

Mochan wheels away in delight after netting the opening goal in Celtic's 3-0 win at Easter Road in April 1954. The win clinched the first League title in sixteen years.

Sean Fallon, a reliable full-back and sometime centre forward, scores Celtic's winner in the 1954 Scottish Cup Final. Aberdeen's defenders were left stranded by Willie Fernie's clever run and cutback from the byline.

Bobby Collins nips in to score against Rangers in a rare 3-2 win at Ibrox in September 1957. Valentine and Ritchie, the goalkeeper, can do nothing.

CELTIC

Official *Programme*

An Appeal

The Directors of Rangers Football Club and Celtic Football Club are very seriously perturbed by the fact that in recent years the games between the Clubs have been spoiled by the misbehaviour of certain spectators, and they now make a very earnest appeal to all their followers to do everything in their power to prevent any kind of disturbance in the future and to assist the Police in every manner possible.

Robert Kelly,
Chairman.

John F. Wilson,
Chairman.

SCOTTISH LEAGUE DIV. "A"

CELTIC v RANGERS

Friday, 1st January, 1954

Kick-off 2 p.m.

Hardly a contender for Programme Cover of the Year. The appeal was made in the wake of crowd disturbances at recent Old Firm matches.

Celtic won this particular encounter 1-0 through this Neil Mochan goal (below) in the second half, but the match passed off without any major incident on the terracings.

Jock Stein, Celtic captain, leads out his team. After joining Celtic in 1951 from Welsh non-league football in Llanelly, Stein skippered Celtic to unexpected victory in the Coronation Cup in 1953 and the Scottish Cup and League double in 1954. Celtic chairman Bob Kelly admitted his own surprise at Stein's success when he told the *Sunday Express*, 'I will be frank about Stein. We signed him without any expectation that he would ever play in the first team.' (9 May 1954)

Jock Stein challenges Derek Grierson of Rangers in the 1955 Ne'erday fixture.

As part of the pre-season training in 1954, Celtic players ran up Ben Lomond. The idea originated from the club's secretary Desmond White, a keen mountaineer, who also took part in the exercise. Depicted here are the first group of players to reach the summit. From left to right: Bobby Evans, Sean Fallon, Bobby Collins and Hugh Fletcher.

Celtic's line-up against Falkirk in a League Cup tie won by 5-1 at Celtic Park in August 1955. Back row, from left to right: Haughney, Fallon, Bonnar, Evans, Stein, Peacock. Front row: Collins, Fernie, Walsh, Tully, Mochan.

Celtic at the start of 1956/57. Back row, left to right: Craig, Meechan, Jack, Bonnar, Evans, Haughney, Fallon. Middle row: W. Johnstone (Trainer), Goldie, Boden, Walsh, McCreadie, Auld, MacKay, McAlindon, J. McGrory (Manager), J. Gribben (Assistant Trainer). Front row: Ryan, Fernie, Collins, Peacock, McPhail (B.), Tully, Mochan. During this season Celtic won the League Cup for the first time, defeating Partick Thistle by 3-0 in a replayed final.

Bobby Evans holds the League Cup aloft after Celtic's 3-0 victory over Partick Thistle in a replay in October 1956 had ended a decade of failure in the competition.

Willie Fernie, a tremendous all-round player. Playing at right half, he makes a determined challenge on a Kilmarnock forward.

Bobby Collins hooks Celtic's third goal in the Scottish Cup thriller at Parkhead on 16 February 1957. Niven, Caldow and Shearer are helpless to prevent the goal but Rangers fought back to earn a 4-4 draw.

John Higgins (bottom of the picture) nets Celtic's opening goal in their 2-0 victory over Rangers at Ibrox in the Scottish Cup replay in February 1957.

and now REX at Hampden

'GERS WERE LUCKY NOT TO LOSE TEN

Supporters for Bobby

A PITY you can't take what you dish out — I refer to Bobby EVANS' honest criticism of the Scottish Press. The Celt is correct. I regard all football reporters, yourself included, as the greatest of all hypocrites and a menace to the game. The recent KICHENBRAND controversy was a classic example of the perfidy of the football Press. A few years ago when Billy HOULISTON was bull-dozing through the English defence he was lauded to the skies by the Scottish Press, yourself included, who then criticised "Kich" for the same tactics.

Your justifying of the extra bob on the gate at Ibrox for the European Cup comes ill from a non-paying member of the game. The "Gers" can exploit their huge support without help from the Press. —"The Mermaid," Mill Street, Rutherglen.

✱ Gosh, I must be a proper rascal.

● A FEUD!

MAY I suggest you try a little self analysis—you could be surprised at the result . . . "grow up yourself." This sniping at Bobby EVANS seems to be a personal feud that has been going on too long. After all Bobby's opinion was asked for and given freely—not without reason, I feel sure. — A. Findlay, Clifford St., Carlisle.

✱ Personal feud, my Aunt Sarah. Bobby's looking down at me from the wall of the Den —holding in his arms the Footballer of the Year Statuette I awarded him in 1953. And I'll swear he's winking too!

Your Space Boys

● GOOD SHOW

THE sprightly play of Johnny HUBBARD at Paisley last week confounded the loudmouths who had him on the way out. Davie LAPSLEY, no lightweight, played the wee Ranger fairly throughout. No easy matter in a game that had boos, handclaps and frayed tempers. Good show, Davie Lapsley!—John Robertson, Newlands Road, Glasgow.

✱ Hear, hear. Davie may have lost the pace, but not the place.

● BIG GEORGE

AFTER seeing the impeccable display of craftsmanship put up by De STEFANO in the TV screening of Wolves v. Real Madrid, I pause to wonder. His flicks, passes and use of the open space were a revelation . . . yet this man, the most fabulous centre in the world, was held as in a vice not so very long ago. He was just another opposite number when George YOUNG had him in his sights. How good Big George really was no one will ever know. — "Lion Rampant," Athelstane Road, Knightswood.

✱ Said Stefano to me after the Hampden game: "Beeg Young . . . he blot out the sun. I try to take heem for leetle walk to the weengs. He jus' nod as if to say, 'I see you w'en you come back.' An' he always keep his promise!" A Spanish official said to me: "Young is like Gibraltar on roller-skates. I weesh Gibraltar belonged to Spain again!"

● COACHING

IS it true that Scotland has no organised coaching scheme for youngsters and that we have one man standing by for three positions and another for two in our Scottish shadow XI? Why is it one never sees Scotland's Under-23s or youth teams playing and practising for the future? I picked up a paper the other night in London, and England had picked THREE teams—one against Wales, another Under 23, and a youth team.—Worried Scot, London.

✱ We have teams in these grades too—and play England and Wales regularly. But this is only PART of the matter. These representative teams reflect the club standard. It's in the clubs that the coaching should really be intensified. I agree, however, that we're too slovenly and careless about the whole thing up here. Fellows like George Young and other great players should be utilised more. And we will simply HAVE to get a guiding hand, like Winterbottom or Peter Doherty.

MY SINCERE THANKS . . . to Patrons of the Putting Board in The Tavern, Millport, (per Tom Gillan), for donation of £1 1/- to my Blind Fund.

HECTIC ON WEDNESDAY

WHY the regrettable clashing of sporting dates this week? Three big shows are cluttered together on Wednesday night . . . (1) the Frankie Jones—Dennis Adams (So. Africa) bantamweight Empire title fight at Kelvin Hall; (2) the Under-23's Scotland v. Holland 'national at Tynecastle; and (3) the Rangers v. Partick Thistle Glasgow Cup semi-final.

And all start around the same time. Careless organisation, surely. By the way, the Tynecastle game will be refereed by one of the two Scotsmen on the F.A.'s top list down south, Mr. Alex. Murdoch.

CELTIC 7
RANGERS 1

Scorers:—Celtic—Wilson (24 mins.), Mochan (44 and 74), McPhail (53 and 81), Fernie, pen. (89). Rangers —Simpson (58).

What a Celtic joy day

AND but for the acrobatic Niven—and the wood round the Rangers' door—it might have been double figures:

Don't blame Celtic for "piling it on." They simply couldn't help themselves — so they had to help themselves, if you see what I mean.

This was a Rangers team with hardly one redeeming feature.

THE DEFENCE HAD A GAPING HOLE DOWN THE MIDDLE WIDE ENOUGH TO HAVE TAKEN THE GUARDS MASSED BANDS

McColl and Davis played with the very fear of death in their boots. I don't blame them.

Up front, the heavy-footed Simpson and Baird took too long to do too little.

Murray was simply brushed aside by Evans — and the wingers, from whom so much was expected, seemed content to appear more or less as mourners.

I don't know when I have seen a more disgraceful exhibition from any Rangers team—especially one parading as League Champions and carrying Scottish hopes in the European Cup.

THEY HAVEN'T A SINGLE EXCUSE. IT'S NO USE BLAMING VALENTINE FOR EVERYTHING, AS SOME WERE DOING.

The fact that must stick in Rangers throats is that they were flattened by the very thing they themselves so badly lack—PURE UNADULTERATED FOOTBALL.

Mark that word "unadulterated." Celtic kept playing the BALL all the time. That stemmed from confidence in themselves.

At the first smell of defeat, some Ibrox men adulterated any skill they had with the physical —a desperation that signposts defeat.

There are limits to what the bull-dozing attack can accomplish, apart from a natural distaste in the mind of the spectator.

BUT THERE ARE NO LIMITS TO WHAT PURE FOOTBALL CAN ACHIEVE.

From the very start, it was obvious that Celtic had nothing in their mind but to play that ball — and, if possible, to be first to it.

Contempt

In the 13th minute, Bobby Collins hit a 25 yards "free" that came cracking off the crossbar with Niven, seeing it all the way, apparently hypnotised.

Then Tully dribbled round Valentine and Caldow near the bye-line and crashed the ball against the near post off which it flew right across the goal and past the other post.

Right now, some Rangers defenders shook like they were operating pneumatic drills.

At the other end, Scott and Hubbard raised the Ibrox hopes with an odd flying scurry—only to prove that Celtic were as tight in defence as they were free and open in attack.

Then Mochan forced a corner off Shearer. When it came over, it was weakly headed out. Wilson wheeled round and hooked it fiercely into the net.

Rangers' long-passing thrusts didn't bother Evans and Co. much. And, in any case, it was sticking out a mile that young Beattie was only likely to be beaten by a shot of the unsaveable kind.

A corker

Right on the interval, Celtic nailed their victory down with a corker of a score

An old-fashioned solo burst from Neilly Mochan took the ball down-wing. He cut along the bye-line beating two defenders cleverly on the way, then slammed the ball into the net from an "impossible" angle.

That was the striking thing about Celts. When one type of attack failed to register, they had the men to try another.

Rangers didn't have one forward who suggested he could have emulated Mochan. Certainly neither winger ever threatened to do it.

This was the most valuable goal of the lot—coming just on the break. And before the taste of the half-time lemon had left their palate, Rangers were three down.

Collins hoisted a long, high ball into the goalmouth. No apparent danger. Till McPhail rose above Valentine, Niven, the lot—and nodded almost apologetically into the net.

Celts were now looking a bit taken aback with the ease of their scores.

Rangers now had Murray limping on the left-wing, with

McPhail beats Valentine then puts the ball past Niven from a difficult angle for Celtic's sixth and his third goal.

Simpson at centre, and Hubbard partnering Scott.

And the only thing this proved was that Simpson was certainly more dangerous in the middle than anywhere else. For he threw himself into the air to bullet a great header past Beattie from a McColl cross.

Rangers' wing-halves moved up to the attack. McColl hit the cross-bar with a "free." Then Baird was cautioned.

Penned in

The Light Blues kept Celts penned in for a time, while they weaved this way and that without finding another loophole—then Mochan raced away and forced another corner.

The unmarked Wilson headed it low for goal. Niven fell on it and palmed it out to McPhail's feet for an easy fourth.

You felt Rangers could thrash themselves to fury all around that Celtic goal area and bring out nothing but sweat—while Celtic could fly away, winkle out the obvious short-cuts at the other end, and do the needful.

The truth was, of course, they had a better defence than Rangers, and a much better attack. Just as simple as that.

Eventually it got monotonous. Wilson, after some tricky smooth-football on the right side swept the ball away towards Mochan on the corner of the area. He smacked it and it bounded into the net.

CELTIC COULD DO IT SOLO, DUET, OR TRIO — OR INDEED QUINTET IF THEY FELT LIKE IT.

Instance: the sixth. Beattie clears from hand to midfield where only McPhail and Valentine are located.

Billy wins in the air, hits ground, races away half the length of the field, and pokes the ball past a bewildered Niven. The rout was almost complete.

In the dying moments, Fernie stroked a penalty-kick home for a tackle by Shearer on McPhail after the centre had again licked Valentine and was on a cert.

It's as difficult to pick out a star Celt as to pick out a star Ranger. Celts had eleven, Rangers none.

Only men I felt sorry for in the Ibrox side were the wing halves, who had so much of the commonplace around them.

Every Celtic player did well, none more so than young Donnelly and Sean Fallon.

Fantastic

Willie Fernie was the most distinguished ball-worker afield, some of his fantastic dribbling runs-at-speed tearing the very heart out of the 'Gers.

Evans was terrific, too, and, with Peacock, completed the great hinge upon which the game flowed Celtic's way.

I must pick out the graceful Billy McPhail for a display of centre-forward play, the ease of which was as misleading as it was deadly.

Celtic — Beattie; Donnelly, Fallon; Fernie, Evans, Peacock; Tully, Collins, McPhail, Wilson, Mochan.

RANGERS — Niven; Shearer, Caldow; McColl, Valentine, Davis; Scott, Simpson, Murray, Baird, Hubbard.

Referee—J. Mowat (Burnside).

A PAISLEY ROAR

NOT for years have I heard a crowd roar like the one that rewarded Paisley Pirates at Paisley Ice Arena on Friday night when they came from behind to shatter Brighton Tigers 5-3. Never before has Paisley had a Pirates team that crashed so early into such an electrifying game.

It was their first match in the British competition—and their new player-coach, Bill Simpell, had a dream debut, scoring a wonder equaliser (Pirates' first goal) a few hours after landing from the Canadian plane.

The pace, skill and tremendous fighting spirit of these Pirates will shake any opposition to its back teeth. No wonder the fans left the rink humming with anticipation.

HERE ARE ALL THE FOOTBALL RESULTS

INTERNATIONAL			
Wales	0	England	4
ENGLISH LEAGUE—DIV. I			
Arsenal	1	Birmingham	3
Aston Villa	4	Newcastle	3
Blackpool	2	Manchester C.	5
Bolton	3	Tottenham	2
Everton	1	Burnley	1
Leeds	1	West Brom.	1
Leicester	3	Notts Forest	1
Luton	2	Sheffield W.	0
Manchester U.	0	Portsmouth	3
Sunderland	0	Preston	0
Wolves	2	Chelsea	1
ENGLISH LEAGUE—DIV. II			
Barnsley	4	Charlton	1
Blackburn	1	Huddersfield	1
Bristol R.	0	Cardiff	2
Derby	2	Liverpool	1
Fulham	3	Leyton Or.	1
Ipswich	3	Grimsby	2
Notts Co.	1	Stoke	2
Sheffield Un.	2	Rotherham	0
Swansea	1	Middlesbro'	4
West Ham	1	Doncaster	1
ENGLISH—DIV. III (SOUTH)			
Aldershot	4	Crystal Pal	1
Brighton	3	Coventry	0
Exeter	2	Norwich	2
Gillingham	2	Colchester	3
Millwall	0	Brentford	1
Plymouth	2	Watford	1
Port Vale	3	Northampton.	0
Q.P.R.	3	Bournemouth.	0
Southampton.	2	Shrewsbury	2
Southend	4	Walsall	1
Swindon	3	Torquay	1
ENGLISH—DIV. III. (NORTH)			
Bradford C	0	Oldham	0
Crewe	0	Tranmere	4
Darlington	1	Carlisle	2
Gateshead	2	Southport	1
Halifax	2	Chester	1
Hull City	2	Bury	1
Mansfield	2	York City	1
Rochdale	3	Chesterfield	4
Scunthorpe	6	Bradford	2
Stockport	0	Accrington	0
Workington	0	Barrow	1

Wrexham	3	Hartlepools	1
SCOTTISH LEAGUE CUP—FINAL			
Celtic	7	Rangers	1
SCOTTISH LEAGUE—DIV. I.			
Airdrie	2	Third Lanark.	3
Dundee	3	Hibernian	0
Falkirk	4	East Fife	1
Hearts	4	Aberdeen	0
Kilmarnock	3	Clyde	2
Partick T.	3	St. Mirren	2
Raith Rovers	3	Q. of South	1
SCOTTISH LEAGUE—DIV. II.			
Alloa	2	Dundee U.	2
Arbroath	4	Cowdenbeath.	2
Berwick R.	0	Ayr United	6
Brechin	5	Dumbarton	2
Dunfermline	4	Forfar	2
Hamilton	4	East Stirling	2
Morton	3	Montrose	1
St. Johnstone.	2	Stenhousem'ir	2
Stranraer	1	Stirling Albion	4
SCOTTISH RESERVE LEAGUE			
Aberdeen	0	Hearts	0
Clyde	2	Kilmarnock	3
East Fife	2	Falkirk	1
Hibernian	1	Dundee	1
Motherwell	1	Queen's Park	0
Q. of South	5	Celtic	2
Rangers	3	Raith Rov.	3
St. Mirren	0	Partick Th.	2
Third Lanark	2	Airdrie	1
HIGHLAND LEAGUE			
Nairn Co.	5	Deveronvale	1
Peterhead	1	Inverness Th.	1
Ross Co.	2	Rothes	1
QUALIFYING CUP (NORTH)			
Clachnacuddin	2	Fraserburgh	2
Elgin City	1	Buckie T.	3
Huntly	3	Caledonian	3
Keith	2	Lossiemouth	3
QUALIFYING CUP (SOUTH)			
Chirnside	3	Wigtown	3
Peebles Rovers	4	Duns	0
Shawfield Am.	1	Burntisland	0
V. of Leithen	5	Selkirk	1
IRISH CITY CUP			
Ards	3	Derry City	1

Ballymena	0	Linfield	3
Cliftonville	1	Bangor	0
Coleraine	0	Glentoran	4
Distillery	4	Portadown	1
Glenavon	3	Crusaders	1
SCOTTISH JUNIOR CUP			
Blantyre V.	1	Douglas W.T.	2
Bonnyrigg	0	Ormiston	1
Camelon	2	Crossgates	0
Dalkeith	3	Blairhall	0
Douglasdale	6	Wishaw	2
Royal Alb.	0	Strathclyde	0
Thornton	4	Armadale	2
CENTRAL LEAGUE CUP			
Bellshill	3	Dunipace	0
Parkhead	0	Maryhill H.	1
Petershill	1	St. Roch's	3
Rob Roy	2	Maryhill	0
St. Anthony's.	1	V. of Clyde	2
Shawfield	2	Bridgeton W.	2
V. of Leven	2	Baillieston	2
CENTRAL LEAGUE			
Benburb	3	Blantyre C.	0
Dennistoun	2	Port Glasgow	2
Duntocher	5	Cambuslang	1
Glencairn	6	Ashfield	2
Kilsyth R.	1	Clydebank	4
Perthshire	2	Pollok	2
Yoker	0	Shettleston	1
AYRSHIRE CUP			
Annbank	2	Auchinleck	2
Ardeer T.	5	Troon	1
Beith	2	Irvine M.	2
Dreghorn	5	Ardeer Rec.	0
Hurlford	0	Dalry Th.	2
Irvine Vic.	6	Darvel	3
Kello Rovers	2	Glenafton	3
Kilbirnie	8	Maybole	1
Largs Th	5	Craigmark	1
Lugar Bos	4	Cumnock	5
Muirkirk	4	Kilwinning	1
Saltcoats	7	Nithsdale	0
Winton Rovers	2	Whitletts	2
RENFREWSHIRE CUP			
Arthurlie	3	Renfrew	1
Dunoon	1	Johnstone	4
LANARKSHIRE LEAGUE CUP			
Newarthill	4	Cleland	1

The *Sunday Mail* report of the 1957 League Cup Final.

Sammy Wilson, soon to form a potent partnership with Billy McPhail, scores Celtic's first goal against Hibernian in a 2-0 win in August 1957, which ensured Celtic's progress to the Quarter-final of the League Cup.

Billy McPhail scores the second goal to leave Leslie helpless again.

Billy McPhail nets Celtic's fourth in the 7-1 Final. Valentine, McColl, Shearer and Niven (goalkeeper) despair.

Billy McPhail heads in Celtic's third goal in the 1957 League Cup Final. McPhail went on to complete his hat-trick in Celtic's 7-1 triumph. Sammy Wilson looks on, while Shearer, McColl and Niven are caught out.

Celtic's fifth goal, a fierce shot from Neil Mochan, rages past Niven. Again, Valentine and Shearer can do nothing, while Tully and McPhail prepare to celebrate.

Celtic goalkeeper Dick Beattie is unable to prevent a deflected shot from entering the net in the late 1950s.

Celtic centre forward Alec Byrne lets fly during the 1957 Scottish Cup Semi-final against Kilmarnock at Hampden Park. The white jersey with the shamrock motif was the club's alternative strip for around a decade until 1965.

A Celtic line-up from 1957/58. Back row, left to right: Donnelly, Fallon, Beattie, Fernie, Evans, Peacock. Front row: Collins, Wilson, Conway, Smith, Tully. Insets: Higgins, Jack, Bonnar, McPhail, Mochan. This squad challenged for the championship until injuries to Fernie and McPhail effectively thwarted that ambition. Earlier, the side had crushed Rangers 7-1 in the League Cup Final.

Celtic in 1958. Back row, left to right: McNeill, McPhail (B.), Haffey, Evans, Beattie, Auld. Middle row: Johnstone (Trainer), Peacock, Jackson, Fernie, Crerand, Wilson, Conway, Fallon, MacKay, Mochan, Lynch, Jimmy Gribben (Assistant Trainer), Jimmy McGrory (Manager). Front row: Tully, Divers, Colrain, Carroll, Murphy, Smith, Collins.

Bobby Collins and his wife leave Glasgow after his transfer to Everton in September 1958. Critics pointed out bitterly that the sale of Collins (and Fernie) effectively paid for the installation of the floodlights at Celtic Park.

Bobby Collins, a ferocious competitor despite his small stature.

Willie Fernie (and his wife Audrey) leave for Middlesbrough after his transfer from Celtic in December 1958. With the later transfer of Evans to Chelsea and the retirement of Tully, Fallon and McPhail, Celtic embarked on 'a youth policy' which was unsuccessful.

Frank Haffey saves from Millar of Rangers at Ibrox Park in September 1959. Peacock, MacKay and Evans await the outcome.

Rangers' goalkeeper Niven is well beaten by Celtic's Chalmers at Hampden in the "Old Firm" Scottish Cup semi-final clash. The other players are Little and Caldow (Rangers) and Mochan (Celtic).

Neil Mochan watches as Steve Chalmers' long-range header beats Rangers' keeper Niven to open the scoring in the 1960 Scottish Cup Semi-final. Rangers equalised and went on to win the replay 4-1.

A youthful Billy McNeill and Duncan MacKay watch anxiously as Davie Wilson of Rangers crosses the ball - an incident from the 1960 Ne'erday match at Celtic Park won by Rangers 1-0 with a hotly-disputed goal in the last minute.

George Niven of Rangers gathers the ball safely as Neil Mochan and Alec Byrne hover, hopefully, in the same match.

PAT CRERAND

Street football was still a common sight in districts such as the Gorbals in the early 1960s. Passing on tips in what was once a Celtic stronghold are Pat Crerand and his cousin, Charlie Gallagher. Both these Celtic players lived in the district at the time: Crerand in Crown Street and Callagher in Cumberland Street. The tenements would disappear within a decade or so as part of the 'redevelopment' of the area.

Crerand, a wing half with exquisite passing skills, is featured in this card, published in a magazine.

Celtic under pressure at Dens Park in November 1961. MacKay clears off the line with Haffey beaten. Kennedy and Crerand look on.

Jimmy Johnstone, 'a pint-sized outside right', indulges in a balancing exercise during training with the junior club Blantyre Celtic in 1961. The red-headed Johnstone went on to become a Celtic legend and a star of the Lisbon Lions, as well as a great favourite of the fans.

Celtic's greatest entertainer takes on the Hibernian defence at Easter Road.

Sean Fallon keeps things steady for Billy McNeill during a training session. Behind Fallon is the most renowned enclosure in British football, 'The Jungle'.

Before a league match at Tannadice in 1961, Celtic chose to strip at nearby Dens Park rather than use the Dundee United facilities which were being renovated. United were affronted at the action. Jim Kennedy (centre) enters the ground, followed by Frank Haffey.

Willie O'Neill and Frank Haffey almost collide in a vain attempt to prevent Dunfermline's first goal in the replay of the 1961 Scottish Cup Final. In the background are Charlie Gallagher, John Clark and Billy McNeill. A youthful Celtic side lost by 2-0 to the Fifers, managed by Jock Stein.

Drama at Tynecastle as Pat Crerand nets a penalty kick in the closing minutes to give Celtic a 4-3 win in a Scottish Cup tie in February 1962. Crerand had missed with his first attempt from the spot, but referee R.H.Davidson ordered the kick to be retaken because he had not signalled. Celtic players, left to right: Jackson, Hughes, Haffey, Kennedy, Crerand and Price.

John Hughes is blocked by a Clyde defender (left). Hughes, nicknamed 'Yogi', broke into the side as a 17 year-old in 1960 but was plagued with inconsistency for several seasons. Until Jock Stein arrived, he was employed mainly as a centre forward but the new manager used him more frequently as a left-winger.

This time Hughes challenges Keenan of Airdrie in a Scottish Cup Semi-final in 1961.

Celtic and Valencia line up in September 1962 for the Scottish club's first-ever venture into official UEFA competition. Celtic lost by 4-2 and went out on a 6-4 aggregate after the return leg at Parkhead. Left to right, the Celtic players are: McNeill, Fallon, Kennedy, Chalmers, O'Neill, MacKay, Carroll, Gallagher, Jackson, Byrne, Crerand. Valencia were the holders of the Inter-Cities Fairs Cup and went on to retain the trophy, beating two other Scottish clubs (Dunfermline and Hibernian) en route to the Final.

Steve Chalmers leaps to head one of his two goals in a 3-0 victory over Dynamo Zagreb in the Cup Winners' Cup in December 1963 at Celtic Park.

John Hughes blasts in the other goal against Zagreb.

Jimmy Johnstone scores in 1964 League Cup Final against Rangers. Murdoch and Divers get ready to celebrate the goal but Celtic went down to a 2-1 defeat. Greig and Provan, on the goal line, are helpless, as is goalkeeper Ritchie.

The Celtic party sets out for a European tie in 1964. For their early European sojourns, Celtic invariably used the Irish airline, Aer Lingus.

Four
1965-1967

Celtic's fortunes changed in 1965 with the appointment of Jock Stein as manager.

Before ... Billy McNeill and the Dunfermline skipper wish each other well at the 1965 Scottish Cup Final. Hugh Phillips (Wishaw) looks on.

And after ... Celtic players celebrate the Cup Final victory over Dunfermline which ended a major trophy drought at Parkhead going back to 1957. Clockwise: Charlie Gallagher, John Clark, John Hughes, Steve Chalmers, Bobby Lennox, Bertie Auld and Billy McNeill.

The goal that kick-started Celtic's greatest days. Billy McNeill heads a late winner against Dunfermline Athletic to cap a Celtic fightback in that 1965 Scottish Cup Final.

Left: Charlie Gallagher, utility forward in the early 1960s, but a mature midfielder under Jock Stein. Right: Joe McBride, Stein's first signing for Celtic, proved a prolific scorer. In his brief injury-interrupted career at Celtic Park, Joe netted 86 goals in 94 appearances in major competitions, earning him the nickname 'Mr Goals.'

Donaldson of Dundee saves from Auld in a League Cup tie at Celtic Park in August 1965, won 2-0 by the visitors. Lennox and McBride (making his home debut) watch anxiously.

Jock Stein created a stir by giving an extended trial to two Brazilian players, Inazio and di Sousa, although neither made it to the first team.

Ronnie Simpson in action at Tannadice in August 1967. Gallagher, Craig, McNeill, Gemmell and Murdoch are prepared to help. Simpson was already considering retirement in 1964 when Jimmy McGrory arranged his transfer from Hibernian for a nominal fee, and he proved a wonderful investment for Celtic by gaining international caps for Scotland and a European Cup medal in the twilight of his career.

When everybody wins. Roy Barry leads out
Dunfermline at East End Park with the newly-
won Scottish Cup while Billy McNeill, assured
of the championship flag, leads out Celtic. A
record crowd of 27,816 attended a memorable
occasion on 30 April 1968.

When somebody has to lose…Billy McNeil
requires treatment in the first minute of the
1969 Old Firm Scottish Cup Final. Bobby
Murdoch prepares to discuss the issue with
Alex Ferguson, whose failure to mark McNeil
at a corner kick shortly afterwards led to
Celtic's first goal in a 4-0 rout – and
Ferguson's abrupt transfer from Rangers.

McNeill, encouraged by his manager to go up for Celtic corner kicks, reacts after scoring against Hibernian in a league match at Easter Road. The Celtic captain scored in three Scottish Cup Finals against Dunfermline, Rangers and Hibernian

The welcoming committee. Celtic officials await the arrival of European opposition at Glasgow Airport in September 1966. Left to Right: Sean Fallon, Jimmy Farrell (Director), Desmond White (Secretary) and Jock Stein.

Left: Jock Stein with the 'Manager of the Year' award (which he had earned for the second time) in 1967. Right: Billy McNeill stands on guard as Simpson goes out to clear.

Left: A formidable manager - Jock Stein. Right: A formidable captain - Billy McNeill.

This picture was taken from a July 1968 profile of Jock Stein in the *Daily Record*. Stein is seen here standing in the Celtic Trophy Room holding a replica of the European Cup, perhaps the most coveted piece of silverware ever won by the club. The article quoted Jock as saying: 'I'd like to be remembered as doing equally as well for Celtic as previous managers have done.' Quite an understatement!

Billy McNeill after opening the scoring in a 4-0 win over Rangers at Ibrox in the Glasgow Cup (August 1966). The victory marked by a Bobby Lennox hat-trick did much to establish Celtic's mastery over their rivals, and marked Celtic's first win at Ibrox in six years.

Within seconds he is mobbed by his colleagues.

Billy McNeill receives congratulations from Watson of Rangers after the League Cup Final of 1966.

The league title has been clinched at Ibrox in May 1967. Left to Right : Provan (Rangers), Lennox, Johnston (Rangers), Craig, Martin (Rangers) Murdoch, Gemmell, McNeill and Wallace.

Hundreds of locals watch as Celtic players take the field in Tbilisi for a training session prior to a Cup-Winner's Cup tie against Dynamo Kiev in January 1966. Bobby Lennox, Steve Chalmers and Billy McNeill lead the way, followed by Jock Stein, wearing a tracksuit. Celtic agreed to play in Georgia because Kiev was 'unplayable' in mid-winter.

The Celtic tourists, with Jock Stein and Bob Kelly in charge, enjoy a day at the Aqueduct Racetrack, New York, in the summer of 1966.

CELTIC
CIGARETTES

A superb Virginia FILTER TIP made in the fine tradition of a great Scottish Football Club

---

Now on General Sale to Cigarette Fans in Scotland

4/7 for 20

CELTIC
CIGARETTES

PRODUCED EXCLUSIVELY FOR
THE CELTIC FOOTBALL CLUB

PACKET FRONT WORTH 2d.

Packet Fronts can be exchanged for Goods at
any shop selling Celtic Cigarettes.

From the programme for the 1967 Scottish Cup Final between Celtic and Aberdeen. Smoking was more socially acceptable then ... but it was not the club's first connection with the industry. The *Glasgow Star and Examiner* (27 October 1906) reported that Celtic's recent home fixture against Aberdeen 'was the first occasion on which tobacco and cigarettes were procurable in the ground, and they were sold, we understand, under the first licence ever granted for a football enclosure in this country.'

Sweating it out at training. Right to Left: Brogan, McNeill, Craig, Gemmell, Clark, Wallace and Murdoch.

Celtic fans help with the preparation for the European Cup Final at Lisbon.

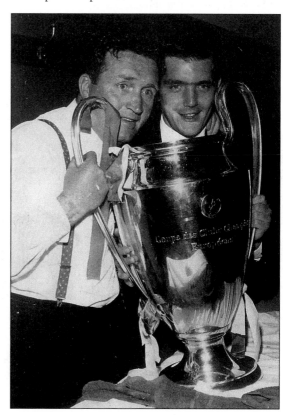

Jock Stein and Bobby Murdoch savour the greatest moment in the club's history.

Celebrations in London Road as Celtic bring home the European Cup in May 1967.

A well-deserved lap of honour at Celtic Park.

FAREWELL MR CELTIC

TODAY (Friday) the funeral will take place to New Stevenston following Requiem Mass in St. Columbkille's church, Rutherglen, of Sir Robert Kelly, president of Celtic football club and the foremost legislator in our national game.

He died at his Burnside home on Tuesday, within a few days of his 69th birthday.

Sir Robert, who had been ill for some months, joined the club as a director 40 years ago, became chairman 24 years ago, and earlier this year became its first president. He had succeeded his father on the Board of Directors; their careers covered the Club's 83-year history.

The Archbishop of Glasgow, the Most Rev James D. Scanlan, described Sir Robert as a very outstanding man. He added: "He was also a man of very great generosity who did charitable work quietly. He was a most devout man in his personal life. His death is a very great loss to the community."

Sir Robert meets the Cardinal.

Sir Robert and Lady Kelly with ex-Provost and Mrs J. Johnston and the Archbishop of Glasgow.

Mr Desmond White, who succeeded Sir Robert as chairman of the club this year, said: "Sir Robert was dedicated to a cause — that cause was Celtic. He saw the rise from a time of shadows to the high noon of success—a success he always believed possible."

Mr John Lawrence, chairman of Rangers, said: "I had a great respect for Sir Robert. Scottish football has lost a great legislator."

James Aitken, President of the Scottish League, described Sir Robert as one of the giants in Scottish football in the post-war era. He added: "He gave the lead in most administrative matters; he was a most outstanding legislator."

James McGuire, president of the United States Soccer Football Association said from New York: "His death leaves hundred of friends here in the United States saddened. He was always ready to help us to promote the game here. We will be forever in his debt."

For more than a generation Sir Robert dominated the destinies of the famous Celtic.

In age of rapid change, the widening of the club's horizons beyond the boundaries of Scotland, the fortunes of Celtic were intertwined with those of its chairman. His career as a director in succession to his father (1931-47) and as chairman (1947-71), both reflected and moulded Celtic's development.

Often, yes, very often, he stood alone as the arbiter of Celtic's future —as the man who sponsored the club's youth policy; as the man who stood alone and defied the might of the Scottish Football Association to destroy evidence of its Irish origins; as the man who fined his entire team when club discipline was broken in an attempt to annex the World Club Championship title in Montevideo against Racing Club of Argentine.

Just as he was the architect of the Celtic which became the first British club to win the championship of Europe and the creator of a domestic set-up which looked after the welfare of former and retired players, so he snatched Scottish football from the grasp of the isolationists.

On all occasions he favoured representative institutions within the sphere of football whether at club level or supporters' level.

He demanded, of course, a stronger and more independent executive power in the chambers of the Scottish Football League and later in the Scottish Football Association and here again Bob Kelly was tops.

When a prominent man dies immediate tributes paid to him are often over-simplified, and the mythical statements that later provoke an excess of revisionism.

So it is best to attempt, even now, an objective assessment of Sir Robert Kelly's public character and record, rather than to remember him with indiscriminate praise. In his case the truth allows more than adequate scope for eulogy, without need of varnishing.

To begin with this sincere man was the finest administrator in the history of Scottish football. A stockbroker by profession, he knew the benefits and the loneliness of a man who spurns opportunism and keeps to principles; he was difficult to know, introverted and sensitive to a degree that caused people to sometimes regard him as an abrupt man.

His concern for essentials enabled him to deliver carefully prepared judgements without notes, and he delivered them with a brevity and sense of timing that no one, in the Scottish scene, could rival.

But though a fondness for fair play entranced him, he was fond of words if economic in the use of them. His "inspirational" periods were good stuff for "show-downs" at the Scottish League and S.F.A. levels but their magic was not of the kind that endures even when translated into print. In that respect some other sportsmen got a better press.

His style was of a wise lucid and savagely humorous judge summing up a fraud case! His elocution was unhurried, but relentless; every word was made to tell.

He took over the presidency of the Scottish League when it was a poor relation of the S.F.A. He brought control of it to the centre of Glasgow, introduced a sense of responsibility for the big clubs as well as the smaller clubs who had dominated it. When his term of office expired, the vice-president due to step into the chair, asked him to remain at the helm until a programme of reforms was completed. This occupied him from 1949 to 1955.

Next it was the turn of the Scottish Football Association itself to turn to him for leadership. At the invitation of the Rangers representative, the late Councillor Wilson, and other Glasgow clubs, Bob Kelly allowed his name to go forward for the office of vice-presidency which would lead to the chair.

Director Park of Queen's Park was the S.F.A. official who canvassed the "renewal" group and it was Celtic's Bob Kelly they elected to lead them. No higher tribute could be paid by the game to a legislator. He had reached such eminence in the direction of the game that it seemed a logical step that he should take on the presidency at a very critical time in its affairs. This he did and from 1960 to 64.

He never forgot that the Club was founded for charity by a Marist Brother. He had been educated by the Marists at Dumfries and his fondness for them never dimmed. *

Celtic F.C. gave more money from its earnings to charities at home and abroad than all the other clubs in Scotland put together.

From the vicissitudes of the game emerged a father-figure who ruled the club from 1947-71 with confidence. This came largely from the practice of beginning each day with a 30-minute meditation at Mass in one or other of the churches on his route from his Burnside home to his office in the city.

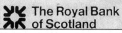

Sir Robert with Sean Fallon, Mrs Fallon and Fr Colman.

Bob Kelly, in poor health for a number of years, died in 1971. This obituary appeared in the *Scottish Catholic Observer* (24 September 1971).

A young girl cries as the Lisbon Lions leave Celtic Park for the last time in May 1971 after a 6-1 victory over Clyde. Ronnie Simpson had already retired but made a brief appearance during the warm-up to great applause from the fans in a ground whose stand was under re-development.